The Environmental Protection Agency

KNOW YOUR GOVERNMENT

The Environmental Protection Agency

Kevin J. Law

CHELSEA HOUSE PUBLISHERS

Editor-in-Chief: Nancy Toff
Executive Editor: Remmel T. Nunn
Managing Editor: Karyn Gullen Browne
Copy Chief: Juliann Barbato
Picture Editor: Adrian G. Allen
Art Director: Giannella Garrett
Manufacturing Manager: Gerald Levine

Staff for THE ENVIRONMENTAL PROTECTION AGENCY

Senior Editor: Kathy Kuhtz
Associate Editor: Pierre Hauser
Copyeditor: Terrance Dolan
Deputy Copy Chief: Ellen Scordato
Editorial Assistant: Tara P. Deal
Picture Research: Dixon & Turner Research Associates
Designer: Noreen M. Lamb
Production Coordinator: Joseph Romano

3 5 7 9 8 6 4 2

Library of Congress Cataloging in Publication Data

Law, Kevin.
  The Environmental Protection Agency.
  (Know your government)
  Bibliography: p.
  Includes index.
  1. United States. Environmental Protection Agency.
I. Title. II. Series: Know your government (New York,
N.Y.)
TD171.G67 1988   353.0082'321   87-33831
ISBN 1-55546-105-0
      0-7910-0862-2 (pbk.)

CONTENTS

KNOW YOUR GOVERNMENT

THE AMERICAN RED CROSS
THE BUREAU OF INDIAN AFFAIRS
THE CENTRAL INTELLIGENCE AGENCY
THE COMMISSION ON CIVIL RIGHTS
THE DEPARTMENT OF AGRICULTURE
THE DEPARTMENT OF THE AIR FORCE
THE DEPARTMENT OF THE ARMY
THE DEPARTMENT OF COMMERCE
THE DEPARTMENT OF DEFENSE
THE DEPARTMENT OF EDUCATION
THE DEPARTMENT OF ENERGY
THE DEPARTMENT OF HEALTH AND
  HUMAN SERVICES
THE DEPARTMENT OF HOUSING AND
  URBAN DEVELOPMENT
THE DEPARTMENT OF THE INTERIOR
THE DEPARTMENT OF JUSTICE
THE DEPARTMENT OF LABOR
THE DEPARTMENT OF THE NAVY
THE DEPARTMENT OF STATE
THE DEPARTMENT OF TRANSPORTATION
THE DEPARTMENT OF THE TREASURY
THE DRUG ENFORCEMENT
  ADMINISTRATION
THE ENVIRONMENTAL PROTECTION
  AGENCY
THE EQUAL EMPLOYMENT
  OPPORTUNITIES COMMISSION
THE FEDERAL AVIATION
  ADMINISTRATION
THE FEDERAL BUREAU OF
  INVESTIGATION
THE FEDERAL COMMUNICATIONS
  COMMISSION
THE FEDERAL GOVERNMENT:
  HOW IT WORKS
THE FEDERAL RESERVE SYSTEM
THE FEDERAL TRADE COMMISSION

THE FOOD AND DRUG ADMINISTRATION
THE FOREST SERVICE
THE HOUSE OF REPRESENTATIVES
THE IMMIGRATION AND
  NATURALIZATION SERVICE
THE INTERNAL REVENUE SERVICE
THE LIBRARY OF CONGRESS
THE NATIONAL AERONAUTICS AND
  SPACE ADMINISTRATION
THE NATIONAL ARCHIVES AND
  RECORDS ADMINISTRATION
THE NATIONAL FOUNDATION ON
  THE ARTS AND HUMANITIES
THE NATIONAL PARK SERVICE
THE NATIONAL SCIENCE FOUNDATION
THE NUCLEAR REGULATORY COMMISSION
THE PEACE CORPS
THE PRESIDENCY
THE PUBLIC HEALTH SERVICE
THE SECURITIES AND
  EXCHANGE COMMISSION
THE SENATE
THE SMALL BUSINESS
  ADMINISTRATION
THE SMITHSONIAN
THE SUPREME COURT
THE TENNESSEE VALLEY AUTHORITY
THE U.S. ARMS CONTROL AND
  DISARMAMENT AGENCY
THE U.S. COAST GUARD
THE U.S. CONSTITUTION
THE U.S. FISH AND WILDLIFE SERVICE
THE U.S. INFORMATION AGENCY
THE U.S. MARINE CORPS
THE U.S. MINT
THE U.S. POSTAL SERVICE
THE U.S. SECRET SERVICE
THE VETERANS ADMINISTRATION

CHELSEA HOUSE PUBLISHERS

INTRODUCTION

Government: Crises of Confidence

Arthur M. Schlesinger, jr.

From the start, Americans have regarded their government with a mixture of reliance and mistrust. The men who founded the republic did not doubt the indispensability of government. "If men were angels," observed the 51st Federalist Paper, "no government would be necessary." But men are not angels. Because human beings are subject to wicked as well as to noble impulses, government was deemed essential to assure freedom and order.

At the same time, the American revolutionaries knew that government could also become a source of injury and oppression. The men who gathered in Philadelphia in 1787 to write the Constitution therefore had two purposes in mind. They wanted to establish a strong central authority and to limit that central authority's capacity to abuse its power.

To prevent the abuse of power, the Founding Fathers wrote two basic principles into the new Constitution. The principle of federalism divided power between the state governments and the central authority. The principle of the separation of powers subdivided the central authority itself into three branches—the executive, the legislative, and the judiciary—so that "each may be a check on the other." The *Know Your Government* series focuses on the major executive departments and agencies in these branches of the federal government.

7

The Constitution did not plan the executive branch in any detail. After vesting the executive power in the president, it assumed the existence of "executive departments" without specifying what these departments should be. Congress began defining their functions in 1789 by creating the Departments of State, Treasury, and War. The secretaries in charge of these departments made up President Washington's first cabinet. Congress also provided for a legal officer, and President Washington soon invited the attorney general, as he was called, to attend cabinet meetings. As need required, Congress created more executive departments.

Setting up the cabinet was only the first step in organizing the American state. With almost no guidance from the Constitution, President Washington, seconded by Alexander Hamilton, his brilliant secretary of the treasury, equipped the infant republic with a working administrative structure. The Federalists believed in both executive energy and executive accountability and set high standards for public appointments. The Jeffersonian opposition had less faith in strong government and preferred local government to the central authority. But when Jefferson himself became president in 1801, although he set out to change the direction of policy, he found no reason to alter the framework the Federalists had erected.

By 1801 there were about 3,000 federal civilian employees in a nation of a little more than 5 million people. Growth in territory and population steadily enlarged national responsibilities. Thirty years later, when Jackson was president, there were more than 11,000 government workers in a nation of 13 million. The federal establishment was increasing at a faster rate than the population.

Jackson's presidency brought significant changes in the federal service. He believed that the executive branch contained too many officials who saw their jobs as "species of property" and as "a means of promoting individual interest." Against the idea of a permanent service based on life tenure, Jackson argued for the periodic redistribution of federal offices, contending that this was the democratic way and that official duties could be made "so plain and simple that men of intelligence may readily qualify themselves for their performance." He called this policy rotation-in-office. His opponents called it the spoils system.

In fact, partisan legend exaggerated the extent of Jackson's removals. More than 80 percent of federal officeholders retained their jobs. Jackson discharged no larger a proportion of government workers than Jefferson had done a generation earlier. But the rise in these years of mass political parties gave federal patronage new importance as a means of building the party and of rewarding activists. Jackson's successors were less restrained in the distribution of spoils. As the federal establishment grew—to nearly 40,000 by 1861—the politicization of the public service excited increasing concern.

After the Civil War the spoils system became a major political issue. High-minded men condemned it as the root of all political evil. The spoilsmen, said the British commentator James Bryce, "have distorted and depraved the mechanism of politics." Patronage, by giving jobs to unqualified, incompetent, and dishonest persons, lowered the standards of public service and nourished corrupt political machines. Office-seekers pursued presidents and cabinet secretaries without mercy. "Patronage," said Ulysses S. Grant after his presidency, "is the bane of the presidential office." "Every time I appoint someone to office," said another political leader, "I make a hundred enemies and one ingrate." George William Curtis, the president of the National Civil Service Reform League, summed up the indictment. He said,

> The theory which perverts public trusts into party spoils, making public
> employment dependent upon personal favor and not on proved merit,
> necessarily ruins the self-respect of public employees, destroys the
> function of party in a republic, prostitutes elections into a desperate
> strife for personal profit, and degrades the national character by lower-
> ing the moral tone and standard of the country.

The object of civil service reform was to promote efficiency and honesty in the public service and to bring about the ethical regeneration of public life. Over bitter opposition from politicians, the reformers in 1883 passed the Pendleton Act, establishing a bipartisan Civil Service Commission, competitive examinations, and appointment on merit. The Pendleton Act also gave the president authority to extend by executive order the number of "classified" jobs—that is, jobs subject to the merit system. The act applied initially only to about 14,000 of the more than 100,000 federal positions. But by the end of the 19th century 40 percent of federal jobs had moved into the classified category.

Civil service reform was in part a response to the growing complexity of American life. As society grew more organized and problems more technical, official duties were no longer so plain and simple that any person of intelligence could perform them. In public service, as in other areas, the all-round man was yielding ground to the expert, the amateur to the professional. The excesses of the spoils system thus provoked the counter-ideal of scientific public administration, separate from politics and, as far as possible, insulated against it.

The cult of the expert, however, had its own excesses. The idea that administration could be divorced from policy was an illusion. And in the realm of policy, the expert, however much segregated from partisan politics, can

9

never attain perfect objectivity. He remains the prisoner of his own set of values. It is these values rather than technical expertise that determine fundamental judgments of public policy. To turn over such judgments to experts, moreover, would be to abandon democracy itself; for in a democracy final decisions must be made by the people and their elected representatives. "The business of the expert," the British political scientist Harold Laski rightly said, "is to be on tap and not on top."

Politics, however, were deeply ingrained in American folkways. This meant intermittent tension between the presidential government, elected every four years by the people, and the permanent government, which saw presidents come and go while it went on forever. Sometimes the permanent government knew better than its political masters; sometimes it opposed or sabotaged valuable new initiatives. In the end a strong president with effective cabinet secretaries could make the permanent government responsive to presidential purpose, but it was often an exasperating struggle.

The struggle within the executive branch was less important, however, than the growing impatience with bureaucracy in society as a whole. The 20th century saw a considerable expansion of the federal establishment. The Great Depression and the New Deal led the national government to take on a variety of new responsibilities. The New Deal extended the federal regulatory apparatus. By 1940, in a nation of 130 million people, the number of federal workers for the first time passed the 1 million mark. The Second World War brought federal civilian employment to 3.8 million in 1945. With peace, the federal establishment declined to around 2 million by 1950. Then growth resumed, reaching 2.8 million by the 1980s.

The New Deal years saw rising criticism of "big government" and "bureaucracy." Businessmen resented federal regulation. Conservatives worried about the impact of paternalistic government on individual self-reliance, on community responsibility, and on economic and personal freedom. The nation in effect renewed the old debate between Hamilton and Jefferson in the early republic, although with an ironic exchange of positions. For the Hamiltonian constituency, the "rich and well-born," once the advocate of affirmative government, now condemned government intervention, while the Jeffersonian constituency, the plain people, once the advocate of a weak central government and of states' rights, now favored government intervention.

In the 1980s, with the presidency of Ronald Reagan, the debate has burst out with unusual intensity. According to conservatives, government intervention abridges liberty, stifles enterprise, and is inefficient, wasteful, and arbitrary. It disturbs the harmony of the self-adjusting market and creates worse troubles than it solves. Get government off our backs, according to the popular cliché, and our problems will solve themselves. When government is necessary, let it be at the local level, close to the people. Above all, stop the inexorable growth of the federal government.

In fact, for all the talk about the "swollen" and "bloated" bureaucracy, the federal establishment has not been growing as inexorably as many Americans seem to believe. In 1949, it consisted of 2.1 million people. Thirty years later, while the country had grown by 70 million, the federal force had grown only by 750,000. Federal workers were a smaller percentage of the population in 1985 than they were in 1955—or in 1940. The federal establishment, in short, has not kept pace with population growth. Moreover, national defense and the postal service account for 60 percent of federal employment.

Why then the widespread idea about the remorseless growth of government? It is partly because in the 1960s the national government assumed new and intrusive functions: affirmative action in civil rights, environmental protection, safety and health in the workplace, community organization, legal aid to the poor. Although this enlargement of the federal regulatory role was accompanied by marked growth in the size of government on all levels, the expansion has taken place primarily in state and local government. Whereas the federal force increased by only 27 percent in the 30 years after 1950, the state and local government force increased by an astonishing 212 percent.

Despite the statistics, the conviction flourishes in some minds that the national government is a steadily growing behemoth swallowing up the liberties of the people. The foes of Washington prefer local government, feeling it is closer to the people and therefore allegedly more responsive to popular needs. Obviously there is a great deal to be said for settling local questions locally. But local government is characteristically the government of the locally powerful. Historically, the way the locally powerless have won their human and constitutional rights has often been through appeal to the national government. The national government has vindicated racial justice against local bigotry, defended the Bill of Rights against local vigilantism, and protected natural resources against local greed. It has civilized industry and secured the rights of labor organizations. Had the states' rights creed prevailed, there would perhaps still be slavery in the United States.

The national authority, far from diminishing the individual, has given most Americans more personal dignity and liberty than ever before. The individual freedoms destroyed by the increase in national authority have been in the main the freedom to deny black Americans their rights as citizens; the freedom to put small children to work in mills and immigrants in sweatshops; the freedom to pay starvation wages, require barbarous working hours, and permit squalid working conditions; the freedom to deceive in the sale of goods and securities; the freedom to pollute the environment—all freedoms that, one supposes, a civilized nation can readily do without.

"Statements are made," said President John F. Kennedy in 1963, "labelling the Federal Government an outsider, an intruder, an adversary. . . . The United States Government is not a stranger or not an enemy. It is the people of fifty states joining in a national effort. . . . Only a great national effort by a great people working together can explore the mysteries of space, harvest the products at the bottom of the ocean, and mobilize the human, natural, and material resources of our lands."

So an old debate continues. However, Americans are of two minds. When pollsters ask large, spacious questions—Do you think government has become too involved in your lives? Do you think government should stop regulating business?—a sizable majority opposes big government. But when asked specific questions about the practical work of government—Do you favor social security? unemployment compensation? Medicare? health and safety standards in factories? environmental protection? government guarantee of jobs for everyone seeking employment? price and wage controls when inflation threatens?—a sizable majority approves of intervention.

In general, Americans do not want less government. What they want is more efficient government. They want government to do a better job. For a time in the 1970s, with Vietnam and Watergate, Americans lost confidence in the national government. In 1964, more than three-quarters of those polled had thought the national government could be trusted to do right most of the time. By 1980 only one-quarter was prepared to offer such trust. But by 1984 trust in the federal government to manage national affairs had climbed back to 45 percent.

Bureaucracy is a term of abuse. But it is impossible to run any large organization, whether public or private, without a bureaucracy's division of labor and hierarchy of authority. And we live in a world of large organizations. Without bureaucracy modern society would collapse. The problem is not to abolish bureaucracy, but to make it flexible, efficient, and capable of innovation.

Two hundred years after the drafting of the Constitution, Americans still regard government with a mixture of reliance and mistrust—a good combination. Mistrust is the best way to keep government reliable. Informed criticism is the means of correcting governmental inefficiency, incompetence, and arbitrariness; that is, of best enabling government to play its essential role. For without government, we cannot attain the goals of the Founding Fathers. Without an understanding of government, we cannot have the informed criticism that makes government do the job right. It is the duty of every American citizen to know our government—which is what this series is all about.

EPA employees collect test samples from storage drums at a former paint factory in Pennsylvania. Agency workers assist local authorities during emergencies and study contaminated sites when requested.

ONE

The EPA in Action

In the late 1960s, owners of a clay quarry in the small community of North East, Maryland, allowed a chemical company to dispose of hazardous waste there. Approximately 1,300 55-gallon drums of chemicals were stacked in the quarry and covered with soil. The quarry was later sold, but the buried waste was never mentioned.

When the new owners began preparing the land to expand their nearby mobile-home community in 1980–81, they encountered chemical odors and leaking drums at the surface. They complained to local and state government officials. Tests by the Maryland Office of Environmental Programs showed that drinking water from local wells was safe, but that organic solvents—chemicals that included several known or suspected cancer-causing agents—were contaminating the surface water and soil in the area. The state of Maryland contacted the United States Environmental Protection Agency (EPA) for assistance.

EPA investigators uncovered drums leaking hazardous waste only a few hundred feet from the trailer park. The soil, two small ponds, and a creek running through the trailer park were contaminated. The situation required emergency action, and the EPA approved an immediate cleanup of the site.

15

*An EPA mobile filtration unit is positioned to begin cleaning a con-
taminated body of water near an abandoned chemical plant in Indiana. Heavy rains created dangerous runoffs at the site and
threatened the surrounding area.*

Work began on June 16, 1982. The EPA and state workers fenced in the
area to keep unauthorized persons off the contaminated soil, removed four
drums of flammable and leaking chemicals at the surface, and used magneto-
meters (metal-detecting instruments) and ground-penetrating radar devices to
search for other drums. Throughout the work, air, soil, and water samples
were taken to determine the extent of contamination. The underground search
revealed that about 125 drums were buried at the site. Because the contents
were potentially dangerous to nearby residents, the EPA decided to remove
these drums without delay. But during the removal, workers discovered that
the 125 drums were only a top layer. In fact, there were 10 times that many—
almost 1,300 drums of hazardous waste, stacked in layers as many as 15 drums
deep.

It was now November. Working against a self-imposed December 16
deadline, the EPA acted swiftly to hire more federal, state, and local
government workers and private contractors. Removal procedures were
streamlined both to speed up work and to hold down the cost of dealing with

10 times more waste than expected. For example, compatible chemicals were combined and hauled off in large-capacity tank trucks rather than in the separate drums. In all, the EPA removed 50,000 gallons of liquid chemical waste and 5 million pounds of contaminated soil, and treated more than 100,000 gallons of contaminated water. After the drums were removed, workers lined the excavation with clay to prevent water from seeping in or out, filled it with clean soil and rock, and capped it with clay. They then covered the site with a layer of topsoil and seeded it with grass to prevent soil erosion. The total cost, $960,000, was only about $300,000 more than the expected cost of dealing with only 125 barrels. It was paid by the $1.6 billion Superfund, an EPA program specifically intended for emergency cleanup and removal of hazardous waste dumps and spills. The state of Maryland installed soil- and water-monitoring stations at the site. To date, all samples taken at these stations have been free of the chemical contamination originally found there.

This incident illustrates how the Environmental Protection Agency handles one of its major responsibilities—to work with state and local governments to clean up hazardous waste that threatens public health. But the EPA does much more.

Created by an executive order of President Richard M. Nixon in 1970, the EPA is the federal government's largest regulatory agency. Its responsibilities, which cover the entire range of environmental problems, are suggested by some of the regulatory legislation that the agency enforces: the Clean Air Act, the Clean Water Act, the Safe Drinking Water Act, the Resource Conservation Act, the Noise Control Act, the Toxic Substances Control Act, and the Federal Insecticide, Fungicide, and Rodenticide Act.

The EPA's history, though short, has been stormy. From the beginning, the agency has been involved in controversies over not only environmental, but political and economic issues as well. It has weathered scandals, firings, and resignations of administrators and directors, as well as major changes in its programs and authority. From a staff of approximately 8,000 people and a budget of about $455 million in 1972, the EPA grew to a high of almost 13,000 employees and a $1.35 billion budget by 1980. But in 1981, the administration of President Ronald Reagan began severely cutting staffing and funding levels. From 1981 to 1983, these cuts reduced the EPA's budget by 30 percent and the number of employees by 23 percent. Beginning in 1983, the cuts slowed, but they continued to hamper the agency's ability to do its job—to protect our environment from pollution.

Despite the cuts and controversies, the EPA has made some important progress against pollution. Working with a concerned and committed Congress

17

A traffic sign alerts motorists to smog conditions on the Santa Monica Freeway in California. The EPA works with state and local governments to reduce air pollution in major cities throughout the country.

in the 1970s, it was able to set standards for clean water and air, regulate the handling and disposal of toxic substances and hazardous waste, and accomplish measures to help control noise pollution. Throughout the decade, Congress and the EPA learned how to work with business and industry to balance the benefits of often costly environmental protection programs against the need for a stable and productive economy. Even though changes in the 1980s have threatened the EPA and many of the antipollution programs enacted in the 1970s, most of its programs remain in force, and the EPA continues to work for a cleaner environment for everyone.

A nuclear power plant in Washington state. Radioactive waste from nuclear plants may be a serious threat to humankind. Some believe that scientists do not know how to store these substances safely.

TWO

The Pollution Problem

Pollution is the contamination of the environment by human activities that produce wastes harmful to life—any kind of life, including humans, plants, animals, insects, and the small organisms that exist in the soil and water. Harmful wastes may disturb the ecological balance (the relationship of all living things to their physical environment and to each other), locally or over a large region, as in the case of acid rain. Certainly a major catastrophe like a large-scale nuclear war would produce such vast amounts of ash, radiation, and other pollutants that the entire global environment would be affected for decades, and perhaps forever. Though we have so far avoided that kind of disaster, there is much concern that some present-day activities are creating pollution with cumulative, worldwide environmental effects. One example is the alteration of the ozone balance in the atmosphere. Ozone is a bluish gas formed naturally in the upper atmosphere. The gas and sunlight react chemically with atmosphere that has been polluted—by automobile exhaust, for example—to form smog, an unhealthy fog. The imbalance in the air created by smog eventually harms plant, animal, and human life.

The contamination of the earth's elements—air, water, and soil—is not new. By medieval times many European cities were so densely populated that the daily accumulation of sewage and garbage could not be adequately disposed of;

such refuse became a major cause of disease and death. From about 1750 onward, during the Industrial Revolution, the ever-increasing use of combustible fuels—wood, coal, and later petroleum products—to produce power for factories spewed tons of contaminants into the air every day, while waste products from manufacturing increasingly polluted the soil and water in industrial areas. One result was the horrible living conditions in factory towns so vividly described in the novels of Charles Dickens and other concerned 19th-century writers.

In the 20th century, the use of insecticides and artificial fertilizers spread throughout the world; and since the 1940s the production of nonbiodegradable synthetic substances (materials incapable of being decomposed by natural biological processes—for example, the compound PCB used in some fertilizers) has increased considerably. All of these activities have improved our quality of life by making more and better goods available at lower cost, by

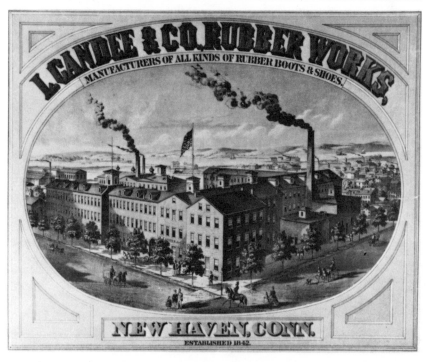

A 19th-century rubber factory in New Haven, Connecticut. Coalburning smokestacks littered the American landscape during the Industrial Revolution.

controlling some causes of disease, and by increasing food production. But these activities have also contaminated the environment.

Our awareness of the negative effects of pollution has grown in this century to the point where national and local governments have finally realized that they must create various agencies to evaluate and control pollution. One reason our awareness and concern are greater than ever before is that our ability to detect pollution, and to pinpoint its effects on health, has improved rapidly over the last several decades. New technology gives us the ability to detect specific chemicals in concentrations as low as one part per million—for example, one ounce of an acid diluted in a million ounces of water. Some substances can even be detected at levels of a few parts per quadrillion. (One part per quadrillion—a million billion—is equivalent to the width of your thumb compared to the distance of the earth to the moon.)

Our improving ability to detect pollutants raises many questions, including: What are the long-term effects of exposure to different environmental contaminants? What levels of toxic substances are truly hazardous to humans, or to other forms of life? Are any levels safe?

An understanding of the implications of these questions requires familiarity with the various types of pollution and their effects on human health and the environment. This chapter looks at today's most pressing pollution problems.

Air Pollution

Most breathable air is contained in the first 2,000 feet of the earth's atmosphere. This shallow layer has a natural self-cleaning capability that, given enough time and space, can handle large amounts of pollution and keep the air safe to breathe. But starting with the discovery of fire and continuing to the present industrial age, humans have been releasing ever-increasing amounts of hazardous substances into the air, overloading the atmosphere and disrupting the natural cleaning process.

In the mid-20th century, scientists began warning that air pollution was reaching dangerous levels in some areas—mainly large cities and busy industrial areas. According to calculations made in the 1960s, stationary polluters (primarily factories and power-generating plants) were discharging some 23 million tons of hazardous pollutants into the air each year; mobile polluters (automobiles and other fossil-fuel-powered vehicles), more than 90 million tons per year. (Fossil fuels are fuels that are formed in the earth from plant or animal remains—for example, coal, natural gas, and oil.)

A traffic jam in New York City. Traffic congestion contributes to noise and air pollution; eventually, auto exhaust emissions combine with the atmosphere to create smog.

What is air pollution? Many substances contribute to air pollution. The EPA has identified and established standards for seven of the most hazardous and widespread pollutants, the so-called criteria air pollutants:

- Carbon monoxide (CO) is a colorless, odorless, poisonous gas that comes mainly from vehicle exhausts.

- Hydrocarbons (HC) are released from the manufacture and use of petroleum fuels (oil and gas), solvents (acetone and kerosene), and some kinds of paint. They react in sunlight with nitrogen dioxide (see below) to form ozone.

- Nitrogen dioxide (NO_2), released from industrial smokestacks and vehicle exhausts, reacts in sunlight with HC to form ozone; it also contributes to acid rain.

- Ozone (O_3), formed from the reaction of HC and NO_2, is the main component of smog (smoke mixed with fog), the thick haze that hangs over many large cities.

- Total suspended particulates (TSP) include the visible smoke and soot spewed from smokestacks, as well as smaller, invisible particles that enter the atmosphere, such as particles of ash from electric-power-generating plants. TSP has been linked to a variety of respiratory problems in humans and animals.

- Sulfur dioxide (SO_2), a major constituent of industrial air pollution, is created

24

from the burning of fossil fuels—particularly coal. It has serious, adverse human health effects and is the main component of acid rain.

- Lead (Pb), a poisonous, heavy-metallic element, is found mainly as an additive in gasoline used to keep a car's engine running smoothly.

Besides these seven criteria pollutants, the EPA has set limits on four other hazardous air pollutants: asbestos, beryllium, mercury, and vinyl chloride.

Some of our worst air pollution problems involve ozone. An unstable bluish gas with a pungent odor, ozone is a form of oxygen that occurs naturally in the upper atmosphere, in a layer known as the ozonosphere.

Interestingly, ozone represents both an environmental benefit and an environmental hazard. Ozone in the lower, breathable part of the atmosphere is a major component of smog. It can harm crops, forests, and the health of humans and animals. Because it is a strong oxidizing agent (it combines with oxygen to change the content of electrons in an atom and consequently weakens the atom), it can also damage materials such as paint and rubber products. But in the ozonosphere, ozone absorbs the sun's harmful ultraviolet-B rays—a proven cause of skin cancer—and prevents them from reaching the earth's surface.

Unfortunately, by polluting the air, mankind has been adding to ozone in the lower atmosphere—where it is harmful—while at the same time depleting the beneficial ozonosphere. Ozone in the lower atmosphere is a direct product of

An industrial plant in Houston, Texas, spews clouds of soot while burning used car batteries. Scientists believe particles carried by smoke can cause respiratory problems in humans and animals.

our industrial age. It is not actually emitted by smokestacks and tail pipes but created when sunlight acts upon the nitrogen dioxide and hydrocarbons contained in such emissions. These substances are emitted by millions of sources all over the world, from small sources such as cars and trucks, dry cleaners, and auto-body paint shops, to large sources such as petrochemical refineries. Ozone levels are highest in cities, which have many pollution sources crowded into relatively small areas. The highest concentrations occur during the day, after morning rush-hour traffic has released large amounts of exhaust and while industries using solvent-based compounds are operating.

The continuing depletion of ozone in our upper atmosphere is also of serious concern. Unfortunately, harmful ozone in the lower atmosphere does not move up to replenish the deteriorating ozonosphere. Scientists are studying why this depletion is occurring and what effects it is having on life on earth. Recent studies seem to indicate that substances known as chlorofluorocarbons, which are used as refrigerants, solvents, and propellants in aerosol spray cans, may float up to the ozonosphere and destroy ozone molecules there. Based on this research, some industrialized nations, including the United States, Canada, and 12 European countries, signed an agreement on September 16, 1987, to ban most uses of chlorofluorocarbons. But many other countries, which are not convinced that these chemicals are harmful, have not joined in this ban.

A swimmer basks in the sun on Miami Beach. Air pollution in the lower atmosphere is depleting the ozone layer, which absorbs dangerous ultraviolet rays that can cause skin cancer.

A crop duster sprays fields with pesticides in California. Toxic insecticides help farmers produce healthy crops but also pollute the environment by contaminating groundwater.

Along with ozone, a phenomenon known as acid rain has become another major environmental issue of the 1980s. Every year, about 30 million tons of sulfur dioxide and 20 million tons of nitrogen dioxide are emitted from factories, utilities, and vehicle exhausts. These substances rise high into the atmosphere, where they combine with water vapor and fall back to earth as acid rain (or snow). The greatest amount of acid rain occurs in the northeastern United States, the most heavily industrialized area of North America. It can drift for hundreds of miles before falling to earth. Thus, it affects not only the areas where it is produced, but also areas many miles away. For example, eastern Canada has been significantly affected by acid rain drifting north from factories in the United States. This has been a matter of serious dispute between the two countries for several years, for acid rain has been linked to widespread destruction of forests and to the killing of many northern ponds and lakes by making the water uninhabitable for fish and other aquatic life. Pollution of one part of the biosphere almost always affects other parts as well. This relationship was summarized concisely by the environmental activist Barry Commoner: "The first law of ecology—everything is connected to everything else."

Water is a renewable resource, endlessly recycled through the natural processes of evaporation and precipitation. It is also the most abundant resource; after all, it covers more than three-quarters of the earth's surface.

This Denver sewage treatment plant discharges wastes into the South Platte River. Point pollution is relatively easy for the EPA to clean up, because contamination can be traced to a specific source.

But despite its abundance, much of the earth's fresh water remains inaccessible and unusable. Most of it is frozen in the ice caps at the North and South Poles, and much of the remainder lies underground. Only a small fraction makes up what is known as surface water—the water in streams, rivers, lakes, and man-made reservoirs.

In many areas of the world, a lack of clean, fresh water represents the most serious human-health problem. Fewer than half of the world's people have access to safe drinking water; many also have little chance to wash themselves and their food, utensils, and clothing. This poor sanitation leads to much disease and death from bacterial contamination. In underdeveloped countries that have few or no facilities to purify water, water supplies are often contaminated with human waste or other sewage. Although the technology exists to clean water of sewage—in most areas of the United States, for example, sewage contamination has largely been eliminated—many poor countries simply cannot afford to build treatment plants.

According to some health authorities, the lack of clean, safe water is perhaps the number-one cause of preventable death in the world today. In recognition of this problem, the United Nations designated the 1980s as the International Water Supply and Sanitation Decade, and other international organizations such as the World Bank and the U.S. Agency for International Development (AID) have allocated millions of dollars for water- and sewage-treatment projects in underdeveloped countries around the world.

Even developed countries like the United States face problems with water supply and pollution. But instead of human waste, here in America our most dangerous pollutants may be chemical substances. The EPA has identified a list of priority water pollutants—those that are known to pose potentially serious risks to human and aquatic life. These pollutants include arsenic, cadmium, chromium, copper, cyanide, lead, mercury, silver, and the synthetic-chemical groups known as polychlorinated biphenyls (PCBs). Besides these priority pollutants, researchers also have identified hundreds of synthetic-organic hazardous chemicals—ingredients in everything from pesticides to industrial solvents—in public water supplies. The ever-increasing number of synthetic

A settling pond at a uranium processing plant in Colorado, where radioactive wastes from processing the mineral are separated from water by evaporation. The remaining sludge is transported to official hazardous-waste disposal sites.

chemicals poses a growing threat to water quality—a threat people are now taking seriously.

We risk destroying much of our water supply. For centuries, surface-water sources fulfilled most of America's drinking-water requirements. But as our population has grown, so has our demand for clean water, to the point where surface water sources cannot possibly supply all that we need. Many of these surface water bodies have been seriously polluted and, despite recent cleanup efforts, remain unfit for human use. More and more, we are relying on groundwater—water that has collected beneath the earth's surface.

Large bodies of groundwater—known as aquifers—are tapped by wells to provide water for drinking and other uses. Americans use some 90 billion gallons of groundwater a day: 13 billion gallons for household uses and almost 230 million gallons for drinking. Almost half of the American population gets all or part of its drinking water from groundwater sources, and this percentage is steadily increasing.

As we have increased our reliance on groundwater, we have come to realize just how fragile a resource it is. Unlike surface water bodies that fill with rain, groundwater does not recharge rapidly. Water must filter through layers of soil and rock to become groundwater—a long, slow process. Groundwater supplies in many areas are subject to competing uses; for example, the same aquifer may be tapped for drinking water, irrigation, and industrial use. Some of these uses can threaten the quality and quantity of water in the aquifer and may lead to long-term contamination that makes the water unfit to drink for many years. The many possible causes of groundwater contamination include faulty septic systems (tanks in which continuously flowing sewage is decomposed by bacteria); leaking, underground storage tanks or pipelines; improperly constructed hazardous-waste dumps; excessive application of chemical fertilizers to cropland; and illegal discharge of pollutants.

Most modern water-treatment systems can remove biological pollution (sewage and other naturally occurring pollutants), but many can do little to remove chemicals. People in areas that depend heavily on groundwater, which purifies itself very slowly, may find out too late that a paint factory or overfertilized cornfields have contaminated their underground water supplies for the foreseeable future.

In the 1980s, a new factor was recognized in the problem of water pollution. At one time, many environmentalists believed that we could achieve clean water by stopping pollution coming from sewer pipes and factories—what is known as point pollution, because it comes from a specific point, or source. But

Scattered railroad cars filled with chlorine gas lie sprawled across tracks following a 1978 derailment in Youngstown, Florida. Disasters such as this one illustrate the inherent danger of transporting toxic substances.

today we know that successful water cleanup must also deal with nonpoint pollution—contamination from sources that have no specific discharge point. Sources of nonpoint pollution range from naturally occurring soil erosion to septic tanks in urban areas and runoff from city streets. Farmers, developers—in fact, all of us—contribute to nonpoint pollution in some way. In many areas of the country, nonpoint sources are the main cause of surface water pollution. Growing evidence suggests that they may be affecting groundwater supplies as well. Because its sources are so many and so widespread, nonpoint pollution represents the water-pollution challenge of the 1980s—and probably the 1990s and beyond as well.

Hazardous Waste

As the earth's population continues to grow, so does the amount of dangerous waste produced by civilization. Disposal of these wastes, both bacteriological and chemical, has become a major problem for modern industrialized societies. Because it can affect every aspect of the ecosystem, hazardous waste may be the most dangerous environmental threat of all.

Perhaps the most serious disposal problems involve nuclear waste. Every year, the world's nuclear power plants produce millions of cubic feet of radioactive waste, including some 140,000 cubic feet of extremely dangerous, or high-level, waste containing the radioactive elements uranium and plutonium—two of the most lethal substances known. In the United States alone, more than 85,000 tons of high-level waste have accumulated since World War II. So far, no one has designed or built an absolutely safe and secure storage system for such waste. Because plutonium has a half-life of 25,000 years—about 5 times the length of the recorded history of mankind—any such system would have to provide permanent storage. (Half-life is the time it takes for a radioactive substance to lose half of its radioactivity. So, after 25,000 years a lump of plutonium would be half as radioactive as when it was disposed of, after 50,000 years it would be one-quarter as radioactive, and so on.) Even a small quantity of plutonium remains hazardous to human and other life for millions of years.

Firefighters try to contain a raging fire at a chemical waste dump in Elizabeth, New Jersey. The poisonous fumes eventually covered a 15-square-mile area, including some residential neighborhoods.

Scientists and engineers have proposed many different ways to store radioactive waste. Some of these schemes include burying it deep in granite mountains or beneath the ocean floor, or sending it in rockets out into space. But in the meantime, until a solution is devised, nuclear waste will continue to pile up in storage facilities scattered all over the world. Many of these storage facilities are unsafe, contributing to the growing problem of radioactive contamination of air, water, and soil.

In trying to satisfy increasing consumer demand for sophisticated products such as plastics and synthetic fibers, modern industry generates large quantities of toxic chemicals. In all, more then 30,000 different chemicals have been identified as definitely or probably dangerous to human health and the environment. And each year industry in the United States generates more than 40 million tons of hazardous waste containing these chemicals. According to conservative estimates, more than 90 percent of this waste is disposed of unsafely.

Over the past decades, Americans have become increasingly aware of the problem caused by the careless handling and disposal of hazardous wastes. Three highly publicized incidents helped focus the nation's attention on the problem, as people realized that no place in the country is free from the threat posed by these substances.

On February 26, 1978, a freight train transporting a variety of toxic and flammable substances derailed near the small town of Youngstown, Florida. The crash ruptured a tank car containing 90,000 pounds of chlorine gas, releasing a deadly cloud. Eight people were killed, 183 injured, and about 3,500 people had to be evacuated from the surrounding area.

On April 22, 1980, a powerful explosion rocked an inactive chemical-waste dump in Elizabeth, New Jersey. The resultant fire raged through the plant grounds, igniting many of the 20,000 or so rusted and leaking drums of hazardous substances—including pesticides, acids, explosives, and radioactive wastes—stored at the site. A dense cloud of smoke and toxic gases rose from the fire and drifted over neighboring residential areas, eventually blanketing an area of 15 square miles. After nearly 10 hours, firefighters finally were able to bring the blaze under control. But their efforts caused even more pollution, as large quantities of contaminated water from the firefighting effort ran off into the nearby Elizabeth River.

Not all hazardous waste problems have involved accidents. Some have resulted from deliberate actions taken over many years with no regard for the environmental consequences. The most famous of such problems undoubtedly was Love Canal.

Boarded-up houses serve as a reminder of the tragedy in Niagara Falls, New York, in the area known as Love Canal. Local residents were evacuated from their homes when they learned that the community had been built on land that was once a hazardous waste dump.

Over a period of almost 25 years, starting in the early 1940s, the Hooker Chemicals and Plastics Corporation dumped large quantities of toxic chemicals into an unfinished barge canal—known as Love Canal—in Niagara Falls, New York. When the canal was full, Hooker covered it over with dirt. Later, homes and a school were built on and near the site of the old canal.

By the 1970s, residents were noticing unusual health problems, including abnormally high rates of miscarriages, birth defects, and cancer. Studies linked these problems to the toxic substances, which by this time were rising to the ground surface and seeping into basements. Tests of samples taken from the school playground and nearby homes revealed more than 80 different chemical compounds, at least 7 of them known to be cancer-causing agents (carcinogens).

In August 1978, the governor of New York declared Love Canal a disaster area, and the state offered to buy the homes of all residents who wished to leave. By April 1979, 235 of the 239 affected families had moved away. On May

21, 1980, President Jimmy Carter declared a state of emergency at Love Canal. Another 710 families were thought to be in danger and were evacuated, some for a short while, others for good.

The crisis at Love Canal needed the aid of a federal agency to assess the damage that was done to the environment and to provide assistance for those people affected by the disaster. The EPA, as a result, served the community in its time of crisis and also worked to make the government aware of its obligation to control environmental pollution.

A participant at an Earth Day rally, April 22, 1970, wears a gas mask. Earth Day events addressed problems concerning the deterioration of the environment and heightened public awareness of conservation methods.

THREE

The Birth of an Agency

The United States Environmental Protection Agency was born at a time when the American people were growing increasingly concerned about the health of the environment. By the late 1960s, air and water pollution and general environmental deterioration had become important social and political issues.

This new concern grew naturally out of America's long tradition of conservation—the wise use and management of natural resources. Although many of the country's early leaders considered its natural resources inexhaustible, some, like Thomas Jefferson, who was concerned about soil erosion, saw the importance of planning for the future. Several American writers also expressed concern about conservation. James Fenimore Cooper, author of *The Last of the Mohicans* and other books about American pioneer life, was disturbed by what he saw as the reckless destruction of the country's forests as settlement expanded. Perhaps the most famous early conservationist was New England author Henry David Thoreau, whose *Walden, or Life in the Woods*, published in 1854, is a powerful protest against man's ruthless destruction of nature in the name of "progress."

In the latter part of the 19th century, scientists began to actually measure environmental damage and issue the first warnings against unchecked depletion

(Left) New England author Henry David Thoreau was a 19th-century conservationist who wrote a book celebrating nature and condemning society's materialistic ways. (Right) Walden Pond, near Concord, Massachusetts. For two years Thoreau lived here in a hut he built himself, studying nature and writing about his experience.

and pollution of our natural resources. Faced with this evidence, the federal government took its first step toward protecting the environment—the creation of a forest reserve system that eventually grew into the Forest Service (managed by the Department of Agriculture). By the early 1900s, President Theodore Roosevelt, an ardent outdoorsman, had increased the total area of protected national forestland to more than 100 million acres.

In the 1930s, during the Great Depression, government programs such as the Soil Conservation Service, the Tennessee Valley Authority, and the Civilian Conservation Corps provided employment for thousands on useful conservation projects from flood control to soil erosion prevention.

Although these measures helped protect the nation's resources from depletion, they did little to protect them from pollution. The federal government was very slow to act in this area, mainly because of pressure from wealthy and politically influential business and industrial concerns. Industry knew that increased regulations on such polluting activities as smokestack emissions and wastewater discharge would mean increased manufacturing costs and decreased profits, and so they fought such regulations.

It fell to private conservation groups such as the American Forestry Association, the National Wildlife Federation, and the Sierra Club, which had long fought to protect specific parts of the environment from destruction and depletion, to pressure the government for stricter environmental protection regulations. These groups were well organized, but they could exert only limited political influence in the face of opposition by powerful business and industrial interests.

Throughout the first half of the 20th century, these conservation groups worked alone and out of the public spotlight. But as pollution's effects on health and the environment became widely known, the American people began to take the problem seriously. In 1962, the book *Silent Spring* by Rachel Carson, which discussed the dangers of agricultural pesticides and urged controls on their use, became a national best-seller—the first book on pollution and the environment to do so. By the late 1960s, concerned citizens of all backgrounds were joining with conservationists and ecologists to form the so-called environmental movement and bring increased public pressure on elected officials to seek solutions to pollution problems.

The observation of Earth Day on April 22, 1970, probably marked the peak of the environmental movement's popularity and political impact. Organized by Senator Gaylord Nelson, a Democrat from Wisconsin, and Representative Paul McCloskey, a Republican from California, the event was devoted to the study

A U.S. Forest Service crew plants seeds to replenish an Idaho forest in 1925. During the 1930s, the federal government hired thousands of people to work in forest, water, and soil conservation programs.

of and protest against environmental problems. Large rallies were held in New York City and Washington, D.C., and an estimated 2,000 colleges, 10,000 primary and secondary schools, and 2,000 communities participated in activities ranging from environmental teach-ins (educational programs) to community cleanups. Congress adjourned for the day, and many senators and representatives spoke at rallies across the nation. President Nixon took no formal role in the observation, but he did issue a statement noting that "the activities show the concern of people of all walks of life over the dangers to our environment."

Early Environmental Legislation

Until the mid-20th century, the federal government had taken a very limited role in environmental policy-making. With the exception of public land man-

President Theodore Roosevelt (1901–09) was deeply committed to preserving the environment and worked to pass legislation protecting national forests.

In 1962, biologist Rachel Carson wrote the controversial bestseller Silent Spring, *in which she attacked the use of pesticides and warned about the dangers of environmental pollution.*

agement, Congress generally considered such policy a matter for local and state governments and hesitated to get involved. But the years following World War II finally brought some federal efforts to address pollution, particularly in the areas it most obviously affects—air and water.

America has a long history of legislation aimed at protecting the nation's water quality. The first such law was the Rivers and Harbors Act of 1899, which prohibited the dumping of any solid waste into navigable rivers and harbors. Although this law was originally intended to keep waterways free of obstacles to navigation, it eventually was interpreted as an environmental law.

In 1948, Congress passed the first comprehensive federal regulation aimed specifically at water pollution control. The Water Pollution Control Act paved the way for most of the environmental laws that followed. It gave the Department of the Interior the authority to force water polluters—both private industries and public agencies—to develop and implement antipollution pro-

A sewage treatment plant. In 1948, Congress passed legislation providing financial aid to local governments for the construction of waste treatment facilities.

grams. It also established federal assistance programs to help local governments build sewage treatment plants and to help state governments offset the costs of their water-pollution control programs.

The Federal Water Pollution Control Act of 1956 built on these measures by authorizing federal planning and technical assistance as well as research and construction grants for municipal waste-treatment facilities. Amendments to this act in 1961 extended the federal government's enforcement responsibilities to interstate waters (those shared by two or more states), navigable intrastate waters (those wholly within one state), and coastal waters and increased the funds available for federal construction grants.

In 1965, another set of amendments to the Federal Water Pollution Control Act established the Federal Water Pollution Control Administration. This agency took over water quality responsibilities formerly handled by the Public Health Service, which is part of the Department of Health, Education and

Welfare (HEW). But the most important provisions of the 1965 amendments were those that called for the development of national water-quality standards and timetables for the cleanup of all interstate and coastal waters.

In the fall of 1969, the Department of the Interior began to use the law to prosecute water polluters. Secretary of the Interior Walter J. Hickel ordered hearings on water pollution charges against the city of Toledo, Ohio, several major steel companies, and a mining company. As a result of these hearings, the city and the industries agreed to set up water treatment plants to clean up their waste discharges into the waters feeding Lake Erie.

Secretary Hickel also ordered the state of Iowa to treat all sewage wastes that flowed from that state into the Missouri and Mississippi rivers and encouraged several other states to speed up their treatment programs. This was the first time that the federal government used its power under the Water Quality Act to set standards for a state.

The federal government's first action to address the problems of air pollution came in 1955 with the passage of the Air Pollution Control Act. This law authorized the Public Health Service to begin air pollution research and provide some technical assistance to state and local governments. The next major step was the Clean Air Act of 1963. This act provided federal grants to local air pollution agencies for control programs and for the first time gave the federal government legal authority to deal with interstate air pollution problems.

Next came the 1965 Amendments to the Clean Air Act, which directed the Secretary of Health, Education and Welfare to establish nationwide exhaust-emission standards for new motor vehicles. The first such standards for hydrocarbon and carbon-monoxide emissions, published in 1966, were applicable to most new gas-powered vehicles starting with model-year 1968. This amendment spurred auto makers to begin developing engines that used low-pollution unleaded gasoline.

Another important piece of air pollution legislation, the Air Quality Act of 1967, strengthened the enforcement powers of local, state, and federal agencies. It gave HEW the authority to designate air quality regions—areas of particularly serious pollution—in various parts of the country and to enforce air quality standards for these regions. For the first time, states had to devise federally acceptable air pollution cleanup plans or face prosecution by HEW.

On February 10, 1969, HEW secretary Robert H. Finch announced the first federal guidelines for industrial air-pollution control. These guidelines specified maximum levels of sulfur dioxide and total suspended particulates that could be emitted from industrial plants.

The first government suit under the Clean Air Act came on February 2, 1969, when the Justice Department filed suit in a Baltimore district court to close an animal-rendering plant (a plant that melts animal fats for industrial use) for violating air pollution standards.

Although early environmental legislation focused on air and water, the 1960s brought regulations for other types of pollution as well. For instance, in 1965 Congress passed the Solid Waste Disposal Act, which set up a national research and development program aimed at finding better ways to dispose of solid waste, or garbage. It also provided for federal financial and technical aid for approved state and local solid-waste disposal programs. Responsibility for the program was split between HEW and the Department of the Interior.

The Santa Barbara Incident

Despite its early attempts at protecting the environment through antipollution legislation, it was not until the late 1960s that Congress began acting in earnest to address what had become recognized as a national environmental crisis. Pressured by the environmental movement, politicians finally realized the need for far more vigorous and coordinated federal action to protect public health and prevent irreversible environmental damage. In late January 1969—at the height of the movement—a dramatic blowout of an offshore oil well near Santa Barbara, California, sharply focused national attention on this need.

Leakage from a damaged oil rig in the Santa Barbara Channel became a virtual river of oil by January 31, destroying marine life and washing crude oil onto 30 miles of southern California beach. Officials of the Union Oil Company of California, which operated the well, estimated that before the well was capped on February 8, it had spewed more than 235,000 gallons of oil and spread an 800-square-mile slick (film of oil) over the Pacific Ocean waters.

Conservationists reported that more than 600 birds had been affected by the oil slick. Carl Hubbs, a former marine biologist at the Scripps Institute in La Jolla, California, warned of the "complete destruction of marine life in the regions along the shore for 20 miles."

The pollution controversy intensified when Union Oil Company president Fred L. Hartley was misquoted in the press as saying "I am amazed at the publicity for the loss of a few birds." In testimony before a Senate subcommittee on air and water pollution on February 5, Hartley had actually said: "I am always tremendously impressed by the publicity that the death of birds receives versus the loss of people in our country in this day and age."

As a result of this major oil spill and the attention it received, the government tightened offshore oil drilling regulations. But the public increased its pressure on the government to take even more decisive steps to protect the environment.

First Steps Toward the EPA

About four months after the Santa Barbara oil spill, on May 29, 1969, President Richard Nixon signed an executive order establishing the Environmental Quality Council (EQC). This agency was intended as a cabinet-level advisory group, headed by the president himself. According to Mr. Nixon, it would function as a focal point of efforts to preserve "the availability of good air and good water, of open space and even quiet neighborhoods." The executive order also established a 15-member Citizens Advisory Committee on Environ-

Robert H. Finch, former secretary of Health, Education, and Welfare, strongly supported air quality control programs. In 1969, he announced guidelines for industrial air pollution control that would be instituted across the country.

A county dump in Colorado. Because such dumps were ineffective and hazardous, Congress passed the Solid Waste Disposal Act in 1965 to research and improve methods for eliminating garbage.

mental Quality. This committee's chairman was Laurance S. Rockefeller, who previously had served as chairman of the Citizens Advisory Committee on Recreation and Natural Beauty.

But Congress was not satisfied by the Nixon administration's actions, calling the EQC a patchwork approach to addressing environmental problems that was little better than nothing. In response, Congress enacted the National Environmental Policy Act (NEPA), a law that attempted to establish the first national policy on environmental protection. Nixon signed the NEPA on January 1 as his first official act of 1970 and set the tone for a new era of federal environmental policy by proclaiming the 1970s the "environmental decade."

In part, the NEPA declared:

> It is the continuing policy of the Federal Government, in cooperation
> with State and local governments, to use all practicable means and mea-
> sures, including financial and technical assistance, in a manner calculated
> to foster and promote the general welfare, to create and maintain condi-
> tions under which man and nature can exist in productive harmony, and
> to fulfill the social, economic, and other requirements of present and
> future generations of Americans.

The NEPA created the three-member Council on Environmental Quality
(CEQ) that, according to the NEPA's sponsor, Senator Henry M. Jackson of
Washington, would "play an independent and aggressive role in defining the
threat to our environment and developing programs to combat it." On January
29, President Nixon named Russell E. Train, under secretary of the interior

*Workmen rake hay along a shoreline in Santa Barbara, California,
in an effort to protect the coast from an offshore oil well leak in 1969.
The accident polluted approximately 800 square miles of the Pacific
Ocean.*

and a leading conservationist, as chairman of the CEQ. The president said that the council would develop and coordinate federal environmental programs and policies and would make sure that all federal activities "take environmental considerations into account."

Although the NEPA was opposed by many business and industry groups, it received high praise from conservation organizations such as the Sierra Club, which called it "an environmental Magna Carta;" that is, a great charter that guarantees the protection of the environment.

The Creation of an Agency

The NEPA represented a major step toward control of environmental quality. But the promotion of its policies was hampered by the CEQ's small size and limited power, and by the widely scattered nature of the federal government's environmental protection efforts. At the time, almost a dozen government agencies—including the Public Health Service, the Department of Agriculture, and the Department of the Interior—shared the responsibility for enforcing environmental regulations.

Stating that the government's "environmentally related activities have grown up piecemeal over the years" and that "the time has come to organize them rationally and systematically," President Nixon on July 9, 1970, submitted to Congress Reorganization Plan No. 3, a plan to unify these wide-ranging responsibilities under a single agency, the United States Environmental Protection Agency.

The president did not propose giving the EPA any powers not already given to its predecessor agencies. The EPA was merely to assume responsibility for preexisting clean air and water, pesticide control, and radiation monitoring programs. But he emphasized the importance of bringing under one authority the government's attack on pollution. He said that the present system of that period, with programs spread throughout several agencies, "often defies effective and concerted action." He also said that the "sources of air, water, and land pollution are interrelated and often interchangeable" and that solving pollution problems in only one area might produce problems in another.

Congress approved President Nixon's plan with little opposition. The House of Representatives voted down a resolution to block the EPA on September 28; such a resolution was never introduced in the Senate. Consequently, on December 2, 1970, the EPA was created by executive order as an independent agency in the executive branch of the government. On that same day, the

In 1970, President Richard M. Nixon signed the National Environmental Policy Act, which set forth the first federal regulations on environmental protection.

Senate confirmed the nomination of William D. Ruckelshaus, an assistant attorney general in the Justice Department, as the agency's first director.

In another reorganization plan devised at the same time as the EPA, President Nixon combined most federal environmental, scientific, and data collection functions into the National Oceanic and Atmospheric Administration (NOAA) in order to provide "a unified approach to the problems of the oceans and the atmosphere." In presenting this plan to Congress, the president said that the oceans "are today the least-understood and the least-protected part of our earth," and he spoke of the increasing importance of learning how to use foods and minerals from the oceans to meet growing world demands. On October 3, 1970, the NOAA was established within the Department of Commerce.

The EPA's Responsibility

The newly created EPA assumed responsibility for many existing environmental programs. Water quality programs were transferred to the EPA from the Department of the Interior's Federal Water Quality Administration and the Department of Health, Education, and Welfare's Bureau of Water Hygiene. Also moved from HEW were programs within the National Air Pollution Control Administration and the Bureau of Solid Waste Management.

The EPA assumed the authority from HEW and the Atomic Energy Commission (which has been abolished) to set environmental radiation-

A pile of empty pesticide cans. Upon its creation, the EPA assumed the authority to register and monitor the use of pesticides and to set limits on the amounts applied to food.

protection standards and also absorbed the responsibilities of the Federal Radiation Council.

It also took over the Department of Agriculture's authority to register pesticides and regulate their use; the Food and Drug Administration's authority to set limits on levels of pesticides on and in food and to enforce these limits; and part of the Department of the Interior's pesticide research program.

After the EPA's creation, the Council on Environmental Quality continued to exist as an advisory and policy-making body. While the EPA was to focus mainly on setting and enforcing pollution control standards, the CEQ was to deal with broad environmental policies and overall coordination of the government's environmental regulation activities.

A commercial airplane flies over a quiet residential neighborhood. As problems of noise pollution began to interfere with people's lives, government officials recognized the need for widespread environmental control programs.

FOUR

Growth in the Seventies, Retreat in the Eighties

Building the EPA was a long and difficult process. Dozens of scattered offices and programs and thousands of federal workers had to be consolidated into one agency. But William Ruckelshaus, the EPA's first chief administrator, pulled the agency together into an effectively functioning unit. Throughout the 1970s, the EPA grew steadily. Its budget (excluding construction grants for sewage treatment plants) increased from about $500 million in 1973 to $1.3 billion in 1980.

But these are just numbers. A better way to understand the EPA's growth and development during the 1970s is to look at the environmental legislation passed during this period. For the EPA is only a federal agency, not a legislative body. It cannot make environmental laws; it can only enforce them. Unless given strong laws to work with, it cannot be effective.

Fortunately, Congress also entered the 1970s with a new sense of commitment to environmental protection. As the first major sign of this new commitment, Congress passed two bills in 1970—the Clean Air Act Amendments and the Resource Recovery Act—that formed much of the foundation for the EPA's early growth. And by and large, it carried this commitment through the decade and into the next; in late 1980 the Superfund hazardous-waste cleanup legislation was enacted.

The Early Seventies—A Time of Growth and Influence

Despite prior legislative efforts (see Chapter 3), air quality improvement lagged in the 1960s. By the end of 1970, not one state had complete standards or pollution control plans in place for any air pollutants.

But the creation of the EPA and the adoption of even tougher standards—the Clean Air Act Amendments of 1970—changed all that. One of the most important pieces of environmental legislation ever written, these amendments set specific deadlines for the reduction of certain hazardous automobile-exhaust emissions and established national air-quality standards for other pollutants. They also granted the EPA the power to enforce observance of these standards. If polluters did not meet the standards by a certain date, the EPA

EPA administrator William Ruckelshaus (center) and an aide meet with a Soviet official (right) in 1972 to discuss global environmental issues. Ruckelshaus successfully organized the EPA into an active and unified department.

This Michigan metal-casting plant has environmental control equipment that significantly reduces emissions from smokestacks. The Clean Air Act Amendments of 1970 put pressure on companies to observe air-quality standards or face punishments of fines and facility shutdowns.

could fine them or shut them down, or both. If methods were not available to meet these standards, the polluters had to develop them in time to meet the EPA's deadlines. This last provision helped spur the development of many new technological advances in pollution control, such as emission control devices for automobiles and smokestack scrubbers that clean industrial emissions of pollutants before they leave the stack. For the first time, polluters were directly responsible for controlling their own pollution.

As passed by both the Senate (unanimously) and the House of Representatives (with just one dissenting vote), and as signed by President Nixon on December 31, 1970, these amendments contained a number of new provisions designed to help improve air quality. Specifically, these provisions focused on four major areas: air quality standards, state implementation plans, automobile and fuel regulations, and noise pollution.

In the area of air quality, the 1970 amendments gave the EPA administrator broad powers to determine which air pollutants needed to be controlled and to develop national ambient (the surrounding atmosphere) air quality standards

An inspector conducts an emissions test on a car. The Clean Air Act Amendments gave the EPA authority to set standards for automobile exhaust emissions.

(NAAQS) that set maximum allowable atmospheric levels for these substances. Subsequently, the EPA developed NAAQS for particulate matter, sulfur oxides, carbon monoxide, photochemical oxidants, hydrocarbons, and nitrogen oxides. (See Chapter 2 for explanations of these pollutants and their hazardous effects.)

The 1970 amendments also addressed air pollution at the source—factory smokestacks and vehicle exhaust systems. They gave the EPA the power to set national emission standards for hazardous air pollutants (NESHAPS), such as asbestos, beryllium, mercury, and vinyl chloride, and to enforce new source performance standards (NSPS) that limited the type and quantity of emissions allowed from new and modified industrial plants.

The amendments also required that each state develop a state implementation plan (SIP), detailing how it planned to meet applicable NAAQS for each air control region or portion of a region within the state. They further authorized the EPA to provide as much as 100 percent funding for approved, state air-quality-improvement programs.

In the section on automobile and fuel regulations, the 1970 amendments called for a 90-percent reduction in carbon monoxide and hydrocarbon exhaust emissions in all new cars and light trucks by 1975. They also required the use of pollution control devices on all new vehicles and authorized the EPA to conduct research on low-pollution alternative engines and fuels.

To deal with the newly recognized problem of noise pollution, the 1970 amendments created within the EPA an Office of Noise Abatement and Control to study noise pollution and its effects on public health and welfare. All types of noise were to be studied, including sonic booms from jet aircraft.

By the late 1960s, increased public concern about environmental protection caused Congress to shift the focus of the national solid-waste program from merely disposing of existing waste, to reducing the amount of waste produced and recovering and reusing energy and materials from garbage and refuse—a concept known as recycling.

On October 26, 1970, President Nixon signed the Resource Recovery Act. This act established a major research program—run by the EPA—to develop new and innovative ways of dealing with solid waste. It also gave the EPA the

A polluted salt marsh in Middleton, Rhode Island. As the result of a 1970 federal program designed to prevent pollution, companies must now obtain a permit before discharging wastes into local bodies of water.

Construction workers break up a pavement with jackhammers. The EPA's Office of Noise Abatement and Control studies the effects of noise pollution on people's health and also sets standards for noise levels from construction equipment.

responsibility of providing state and local governments with technical and financial help in planning and developing resource recovery and waste disposal systems.

As the "environmental decade" continued, Congress focused its attention on all major forms of pollution. The early 1970s saw dozens of regulations proposed and adopted as politicians responded to the public's strong desire for a clean, safe environment. In 1970, President Nixon announced a new program to control water pollution from industrial sources. This program, based on the Rivers and Harbors Act of 1899, required that all industries obtain a permit before discharging any wastewater. This measure not only eliminated some sources of water pollution, but also provided the federal government with information on the nature and extent of industrial pollution in this country.

In 1972, water quality legislation entered a new era with the passage of the Federal Water Pollution Control Act Amendments. This bill, the most wide-ranging and expensive environmental legislation enacted to that time, became law only after Congress overrode President Nixon's veto on the last day of the 1972 congressional session.

These water pollution amendments marked a basic change in the approach to pollution control by adding strict limits to the existing water quality standards on what could be discharged into waterways. They also extended federal responsibility for water pollution control to all the nation's waters. Under the amendments, the EPA could for the first time establish nationwide water quality standards and limits on the amount of waste that could be discharged into the waterways. In addition, the amendments toughened the requirements for discharge permits and required that industrial dischargers submit plans and schedules for bringing their discharges in line with federal standards. As stated in its opening passage, this new law's overall goal was to "restore and maintain the physical, chemical, and biological integrity of the nation's waters." It set specific goals of making all the nation's surface water bodies "fishable and swimmable" by 1983, and of eliminating all pollutant discharges into navigable waters by 1985.

Also in 1972 came the first legislation aimed solely at controlling noise pollution. The Noise Control Act of 1972, passed on Congress's last day of session for the year, gave the EPA authority to set standards limiting noise levels from certain commercial sources, including construction equipment, motors and engines, and electronic equipment. It also directed the EPA to propose noise standards for commercial aircraft, but gave final responsibility for setting these standards to the Federal Aviation Administration (FAA).

Earlier that year, Congress had made the first major change in 25 years in the national policy on pesticide regulation. The new legislation—the Federal Environmental Pesticide Control Act of 1972—required that all pesticides be registered with the EPA. This in effect gave the EPA control over the manufacture, distribution, and use of pesticides. Under the previous law—the Insecticide, Fungicide, and Rodenticide Act of 1947—the government had to go through a long and complicated procedure to ban a dangerous pesticide and could not punish those who used such a substance improperly. The new law made it easier to ban hazardous pesticides and imposed penalties for their improper use. It divided pesticides into two categories—general use (considered nonhazardous) and restricted use (hazardous). Restricted-use pesticides would have to be clearly labeled and could be used only by licensed persons. All pesticide manufacturers would have to submit to the EPA detailed information on chemical formulas, directions for use, and safety test results.

Although the Clean Water Act Amendments of 1972 dealt with water pollution, they did not specifically address drinking-water quality. In 1974,

Congress passed the Safe Drinking Water Act (SDWA) in an effort to correct the problem of inconsistent state protection of public drinking-water supplies. Across the country, drinking water quality was uneven; standards varied widely from state to state, and sometimes even in different areas of the same state. The SDWA established the first comprehensive program to eliminate these inconsistencies and set nationwide standards for drinking water quality. It directed the EPA to set maximum allowed levels for certain chemical and biological (bacteriological) pollutants and brought under EPA standards almost 240,000 community water supply systems serving a total of more than 200 million people.

The SDWA grew out of an increasing concern over the health effects of drinking-water pollution. An EPA report issued on November 7, 1974, presented the results of water testing of the city of New Orleans's public water supply. The tests uncovered 66 different pollutants, some of them suspected carcinogens. In a national press conference called to discuss the report, EPA administrator Russell E. Train (who had replaced William Ruckelshaus in 1973), outlined the agency's plans to survey the drinking water in 80 American cities.

Although air and water pollution got most of the early attention, as the 1970s progressed the safe handling and disposal of hazardous wastes also became an increasing public concern. In 1976, Congress responded to this concern by enacting the Resource Conservation and Recovery Act (RCRA). The RCRA set the first regulations for the generation, transportation, and disposal of hazardous waste. Under the new law, the EPA established a registration system that tracked hazardous materials from manufacture to disposal. But although it provided the EPA with the tools to track and regulate the handling of such substances, the RCRA did not address existing hazardous-waste disposal sites and the problems associated with improperly constructed or operated disposal facilities or unsafe disposal practices. The EPA had no authority to engage in emergency cleanup of existing sites. The Clean Water Act enabled the EPA (in cooperation with the Coast Guard), to take action when oil or other hazardous substances were discharged into navigable waterways. But it did not give the EPA or any other government agency the authority to act when hazardous substances were released to other parts of the environment, including the land, the air, and groundwater and non-navigable surface-water bodies. But another piece of legislation passed in 1976—the Toxic Substances Control Act (TOSCA)—did give the EPA broad powers to control the distribution and use of commercial and industrial chemicals known or thought to be hazardous to human health and the environment. The bill singled out for special attention a class of chemical compounds known as PCBs (polychlorinated biphenyls), which are used in electric transformers and capacitors and in many other industrial and commercial products. Like the banned pesticide DDT, PCBs were found to persist in the environment, accumulate in human and animal tissue, and cause major health problems. In 1976, high levels of PCBs were found in the Great Lakes, the Hudson River, and other bodies of water and in fish taken from those waters. TOSCA called for a complete ban on the manufacture and use of PCBs by 1979.

The Mid-Seventies—Some Changes in Direction

The EPA's first half-decade was filled with a strong sense of purpose and excitement over the many important environmental laws passed and the agency's ever-widening responsibilities. In just five short years, the EPA had become one of the largest and most powerful of all federal agencies. But this

A sign at a pesticide waste site warns of hazardous materials. Pesticide manufacturers must comply with safety standards under the Federal Environmental Pesticide Control Act of 1972.

61

situation was not to last. By the mid-1970s, the environmental movement was beginning to lose momentum. The Arab oil embargo of 1974 forced oil and gasoline prices skyward, burdened the American economy, and led to runaway inflation. Faced with new economic hardships, business and industry pleaded with Congress to ease some of the strict environmental regulations that added greatly to the cost of doing business. And members of Congress, no longer as mindful of environmentalists and their concerns—and faced, as always, with the political reality of needing to cooperate with powerful business and industrial interests—began to soften their position.

Some of the most significant softening occurred in regard to the Clean Air Act—and particularly the Clean Air Act Amendments of 1977. More than 180 pages long (more than 3 times as long as the original Clean Air Act Amendments of 1970), the 1977 amendments constitute one of the most detailed and complex environmental laws ever written. Although they preserved the overall goal of the 1970 amendments—to protect public health by cleaning the air—the 1977 amendments extended deadlines for meeting standards and thus delayed achieving this goal.

Russell Train (right) is sworn in as EPA administrator by U.S. Attorney General Elliot Richardson in 1973. Train directed a survey of the drinking water in 80 cities to determine water quality standards across the country.

In their major provisions, the 1977 amendments did the following:

Extended for two years the deadline for automobile
manufacturers to achieve exhaust emissions standards.
Gave most industrial polluters up to three more years to meet
existing standards.
Extended the deadline for cities to meet NAAQS (national air-
quality standards) until 1982, and in some cases until 1987.
[The previous deadline was 1977.]
Directed the EPA to review existing air quality standards
before 1981 and again every five years thereafter.

Congress's most difficult task came in revising automobile emissions standards. Car manufacturers requested deadline extensions, claiming that they could not possibly meet the standards in their 1978-model cars. Industry leaders threatened to shut down their assembly lines rather than produce cars that could not meet the standards, for which they would face EPA fines of up to $10,000 for each car. In response to this threat, President Carter pleaded with Congress to move back the deadlines to avoid potential harm to the American economy.

Also in 1977, Congress acted to soften some provisions of the Clean Water Act Amendments of 1972. These changes—enacted as the Clean Water Act of 1977—allowed some delays in the cleanup of water pollutants for economic reasons, giving polluters more time to implement expensive water-treatment systems or to devise other ways to meet water quality standards. Although lawmakers described the changes as only "midcourse corrections" that would not affect the 1972 act's overall goals, the revisions satisfied neither industry, which wanted a major rewrite and relaxing of standards, nor environmentalists, who wanted to hold to the original regulations and deadlines.

Indicative of the EPA's new willingness to cooperate with, rather than confront, industry, agency administrator Douglas Costle (who had replaced Russell Train in 1977) praised the new law as a step toward reasonable and achievable pollution-control standards.

Although changes to the air and water pollution laws somewhat weakened the EPA's authority in these areas, Congress in the late 1970s did not abandon completely its original goals of a safe and healthy environment. President Jimmy Carter was personally concerned with environmental issues, and the American people still expressed a desire for strong regulations. In the last days of the 1980 session, Congress passed a bill addressing one of the most pressing environmental problems—hazardous waste.

EPA emergency crews work with state officials to contain toxic waste spills at both current and former waste disposal sites.

Superfund and the End of an Era

The Resource Conservation and Recovery Act, the Clean Water Act, and other environmental laws authorized the EPA to take legal action to force persons or corporations who create, transport, or dispose of hazardous waste to clean up any pollution they cause. But an old, abandoned dump site— hundreds, perhaps thousands, are scattered throughout the country—may be impossible to link with an owner or a polluter (see Chapter 1 for an example of such a situation). And polluters are often unable to pay the high costs of cleanup. In addition, an accidental release of a hazardous substance often requires emergency response to prevent serious environmental damage. There may not be time for complicated legal action against a polluter before cleanup must begin.

Although some states had set up their own programs for emergency response and cleanup of abandoned sites, they often lacked the funds and legal authority to address many of the problems.

In the late 1970s, Love Canal and other hazardous waste disasters (see Chapter 2) focused national attention on the problem. In response to public pressure, Congress in 1980 enacted new legislation establishing a program coordinating federal and state efforts to deal with releases of hazardous substances into the environment. This legislation, the Comprehensive Environmental Response, Compensation, and Liability Act (CERCLA) of 1980—popularly known as the Superfund—permits the federal government, under the authority of the EPA, to work with state and local governments to clean up hazardous waste. A $1.6 billion trust fund provided money to pay for both emergency and long-term cleanups of waste spills and active and inactive disposal sites. The funds come from special taxes paid by manufacturers, producers, and importers of oil and 42 designated toxic chemical substances.

CERCLA also required the EPA to revise the National Contingency Plan. This plan, first developed in 1968, details the required steps in an emergency response to a major release of oil or hazardous substances for 14 federal agencies and state and local governments. As revised, it now gives primary

A dead bird lies amid oil sludge off the coast of Texas. The EPA assists with the cleanup of oil spills on land and in inland bodies of water; the U.S. Coast Guard handles spills near coastal areas and in the Great Lakes.

responsibility for dealing with all such emergencies on land and in inland waters to the EPA; the U.S. Coast Guard is responsible for accidental spills in or near coastal waters and in the Great Lakes. In general, the plan encourages the cooperation of the EPA with state and local governments in emergency response actions. It also allows state and local governments to bill the federal government for certain cleanup costs and authorizes the EPA to undertake cleanup when the polluter or the state government cannot or will not do so.

CERCLA, an unprecedented piece of hazardous-waste legislation, brought the "environmental decade" to a fitting close. It also ended an impressively productive period of environmental lawmaking; more new environmental regulations were enacted during the 1970s than during all the previous years combined. But the end of the 1970s also brought an end to new pollution control laws. Although it was enacted as long ago as 1980, CERCLA remains today the last important piece of environmental legislation passed by Congress. Why the radical departure from the activity of the 1970s? The reasons lay in the very different policies of a new administration, that of Ronald Reagan.

The 1980s—An Agency in Peril

The election of Ronald Reagan as president in November 1980 marked not only the end of the EPA's first decade, but also the end of a progressive era. President Reagan and his conservative political aides and allies shared a view of environmental regulation that was radically different from that of the administrations that had preceded him. He believed that although some regulation was necessary to protect public health, the costs and bureaucratic problems of regulating pollution had gotten out of hand and needed to be cut back. He also believed that many of the environmental regulations written during the 1970s were hurting the nation's economy by forcing industry to spend millions of dollars on pollution control.

The Reagan administration quickly took steps to alter this situation. One of the president's first acts in office, on January 22, 1981, was to create the Presidential Task Force on Regulatory Relief. Headed by Vice-president George Bush, this task force was set up to review existing and proposed regulations for all government agencies. In its review of environmental regulations, the task force was to recommend changes that would relieve the regulatory "burden" on business, industry, and state and local governments.

According to the task force, most of this burden resulted from EPA regulations. Among the regulations singled out were those affecting the

President Ronald Reagan supported the softening of antipollution legislation during the 1980s because he felt costs for installing special pollution control devices were an excessive burden on industry and hurt the nation's economy.

automobile industry, particularly exhaust emissions standards and lead limits in gasoline; industrial pretreatment of wastewater disposal; and pesticide registration. By December 1981, the task force had targeted 91 existing regulations for review and possible change. By August 1983, when the task force disbanded, it had reviewed 119 regulations; of these, 76 were revised or eliminated. Many were EPA regulations.

Besides reviewing existing regulations, the Reagan administration introduced a policy for evaluating proposed new ones. Under Executive Order 12291, issued on February 17, 1981, any government agency proposing a new environmental regulation had to calculate the regulation's benefits in economic terms and balance these against its costs. Only regulations that had economic benefits exceeding their costs could become law. This represented a dramatic departure from previous policy, which evaluated a regulation's benefits based on purely environmental concerns. The president's economic program, with its emphasis on cutbacks in government programs of all kinds in favor of a major buildup of national defense spending, had become the guide to all environmental decision making.

In this same spirit of financial conservatism, another important part of President Reagan's regulatory reform strategy involved reducing the power and influence of the EPA (and other regulatory agencies as well), by drastically cutting its staffing and funding levels. Even before President Reagan had hired a new administrator to replace Douglas Costle (whose appointment had expired with Jimmy Carter's defeat in the 1980 election), his Office of Management and Budget (OMB) cut the EPA's staff by 11 percent and its budget by 12 percent. The OMB also proposed a second 12 percent budget cut to take effect just 6 months after the first. By 1984, EPA staff cuts totalled 29 percent and budget cuts 44 percent from 1980 levels. The Council on Environmental Quality was even more devastated. In 1981, the Reagan administration dismissed the CEQ's entire professional staff and slashed its budget by more than 70 percent.

Possibly President Reagan's most controversial action involving the EPA was his appointment of Anne Gorsuch as EPA administrator. A former telephone company lawyer and Colorado state legislator, and a protégé of James Watt, the equally controversial secretary of the interior, Gorsuch had little background in environmental policy-making when she assumed office on May 5, 1981.

Gorsuch took control of the EPA with orders from the White House to streamline the agency's massive bureaucracy, slash its budget and staff, and

Anne Gorsuch Burford at a congressional hearing in 1983. She resigned as EPA administrator after an investigation revealed that EPA funds had been used illegally for some congressional election campaigns.

relieve industry of burdensome and costly environmental regulations. The EPA's new direction quickly became evident, as Gorsuch filled 12 of the agency's 16 top administrative posts with former attorneys, lobbyists, and consultants for industries the EPA regulates. Most had little or no prior experience in government, and not one had ever worked in environmental administration. To concerned environmentalists, the "foxes were now guarding the chicken coop," to quote a popular criticism of these changes. At the same time, Gorsuch made severe cuts in the EPA staff. Total employment in the EPA dropped from 14,269 persons in January 1981 to 11,474 by November 1982, a loss of 1 out of every 5 employees.

By the fall of 1982, the impact of these policies on the EPA was clear. To some political observers, the Reagan administration seemed to be trying not to change the agency, but to eliminate it completely. This was a minority opinion, but even those who did not share it had to admit that the EPA's future was being jeopardized by the deep budget and staffing cuts and sinking morale.

The low point came on December 16, 1982, when the House of Representatives voted to cite administrator Gorsuch—since a recent marriage, known as Anne Burford—for contempt of Congress. She was one of the highest government officials ever to be so censured. Congress took this drastic action because Burford refused to turn over to the House documents on alleged mismanagement of the Superfund program for cleaning up the nation's toxic waste dumps. Over the following months, the newspapers were full of stories detailing arrangements for preferential treatment that Burford and her top aide, Rita Lavelle, had allegedly made with industrial and business lobbyists. As the investigation into Burford's activities deepened, evidence pointed to widespread political mischief, including manipulation of Superfund monies to help Republican congressional candidates' election campaigns, and development of a "hit list" that targeted for dismissal certain EPA scientists who were felt to be unfriendly to the Reagan administration.

By 1983, the scandal had badly damaged the EPA's credibility and effectiveness. President Reagan, worried that the situation might threaten his reelection in 1984, pressured Burford to resign. At first she resisted, protesting that she had done no wrong and was merely carrying out the administration's policies. But finally, in March 1983, she stepped down. Most of her closest staff members soon followed.

In an attempt to regain some of the EPA's lost prestige, President Reagan appointed William D. Ruckelshaus to take Burford's place. It was hoped that Ruckelshaus, the agency's first administrator in the early 1970s, would restore some stability to the EPA. Many environmentalists remembered him as a

Lee M. Thomas, EPA administrator since 1985, has tried to persuade the Reagan administration to toughen its policy on acid rain and the disposal of hazardous waste.

strong and able administrator during his first term and hoped that he would bring that same strength to his second. But others noted that he had strong ties with businesses regulated by the EPA (in fact, he had left an executive position with the Weyerhaeuser Company, a huge forest products combine, to take the EPA job) and wondered if he would be truly committed to environmental programs.

Whether committed or not, Ruckelshaus was able to make some progress in turning the EPA around. By November 1983, just six months after his return, he had replaced all the top agency officials who had been swept out with Anne Burford. He had also been able to convince many top-notch scientists who had resigned during the Burford years to come back. The EPA's morale began to improve, as did its public image. But Ruckelshaus had less success with the EPA's budget. The OMB continued to slash funds for the agency, particularly in the area of enforcement.

Ruckelshaus's environmental record was mixed. In the area of hazardous waste and toxic chemicals, he found that pleasing both environmentalists and the Reagan administration was a difficult task. Environmentalists criticized his decision to weaken EPA standards for several toxic substances, including radiation levels from uranium mills; industrial emissions of benzene, a powerful carcinogen; and exhaust emissions from diesel-powered cars and light trucks. But they cheered his decision to reverse a policy drafted by Anne Burford that would have allowed states to weaken water quality standards in order to promote industrial growth. One of his pet projects, legislation to reduce acid rain, was hampered by the Reagan administration's emphasis on cost control at the expense of environmental protection. Although Ruckelshaus proposed a plan in 1983 to reduce industrial sulfur-dioxide emissions, such as emissions from oil- and coal-fired power plants, the president rejected the plan as too expensive. To date, the EPA has no comprehensive acid-rain-control regulation. The feelings many environmentalists had about Ruckelshaus's second term were summed up by Representative James J. Florio, a Democrat from New Jersey who was a leading critic of Burford and the Reagan administration's environmental record. In late 1983, Florio stated:

> He [Ruckelshaus] is just in neutral. He's never going to do anything
> that's wrong, but this administration's environmental policy is not going
> to be an aggressive policy until Ruckelshaus decides he doesn't want to
> be a good soldier.

Perhaps frustrated by his lack of progress at influencing the Reagan administration's environmental outlook, Ruckelshaus resigned as EPA administrator in January 1985 and was succeeded by his deputy administrator, Lee M. Thomas.

Although Thomas received general approval from environmentalists, many expressed concern that he would face the same problem as Ruckelshaus in influencing an administration that seemed indifferent to pollution problems. Those concerns were well-founded, for although Congress and the EPA managed to hold the line on many environmental programs and prevent further weakening of regulations, many problems—such as acid rain and hazardous waste—remained as serious as ever.

EPA headquarters in Washington, D.C. From this office, the EPA administrator and deputy administrator supervise agency activities and policy for the entire country.

FIVE

The EPA Today

Since its inception in 1970, the EPA has grown to be one of the largest of all independent government agencies. Even with the staff cuts of the preceding 5 years, in 1985 the EPA ranked sixth in total employment among independent agencies, with almost 13,500 persons. Although its headquarters is in Washington, D.C., the agency has a significant presence throughout the country. This chapter explains the functions and responsibilities of the major offices of the EPA and describes how the agency goes about setting standards and dealing with problems of environmental protection throughout the United States.

The EPA's Structure

At the agency's national headquarters, an isolated office complex in southwestern Washington, D.C., the EPA administrator and deputy administrator oversee the agency's activities. The administrator is appointed directly by the president of the United States, subject to Senate approval; the deputy administrator is chosen by the administrator.

Reporting directly to the administrator and his deputy are the associate administrator for International Activities and the associate administrator for

EPA workers use special equipment to collect samples of water for analysis at an agency laboratory. Test results are used in further research and reported to Congress, environmentalists, and local government officials.

Regional Operations. The Office of International Activities (OIA) advises the administrator and other principal EPA officials on the progress and impact of foreign and international programs, policies, and issues, and on the impact abroad of EPA policies and programs. The OIA associate administrator also serves as the administrator's representative in contacts with the State Department and other government agencies concerned with international affairs, as well as with the United Nations, the North Atlantic Treaty Organization (NATO), and other international organizations. The Office of Regional Operations (ORO) coordinates the actions of the EPA's 10 regional offices throughout the nation.

Also reporting to the administrator and deputy administrator are the heads of four specialized EPA staff offices: the Office of Administrative Law Judges, the Office of Civil Rights, the Office of Small and Disadvantaged Business Utilization, and the Science Advisory Board. The Office of Administrative Law Judges deals with interpreting detailed environmental regulations from a legal point of view. The Office of Civil Rights and the Office of Small and Disadvantaged Business Utilization advise the administrator on equal opportunity and civil rights programs and policies, economic programs for minorities, and the impact of EPA programs on urban areas. These offices provide the focal point for the EPA's interaction with other federal departments and agencies such as the Justice Department, the Department of Commerce, the Civil Service Commission, the Equal Employment Opportunity Commission, and the United States Commission on Civil Rights. The Science Advisory Board, a panel of distinguished scientists and academicians appointed by the administrator, advises the administrator on current scientific and technological advances in pollution control.

Eleven assistant administrators head specialized offices responsible for different aspects of agency operations. Four of these offices—the Office of Air and Radiation Programs, the Office of Water Programs, the Office of Solid Waste and Emergency Response Programs, and the Office of Pesticides and Toxic Substances Programs—deal directly with specific areas of environmental concern. In general, these four offices are responsible for developing national antipollution policies, programs, and regulations and for coordinating EPA monitoring and enforcement activities. They also provide state and local environmental agencies with technical and sometimes financial assistance in the development of pollution control systems and strategies.

The Office of Research and Development (ORD) serves as the science and technology adviser to the administrator and is responsible for developing and conducting a national research program on the sources and effects of pollution, environmental sciences, and pollution control technology. The ORD assistant administrator provides direct supervision of the activities of EPA research laboratories and ensures the quality control and standardization of techniques used by the EPA's regional support laboratories. He also exercises planning, coordinating, and evaluating responsibilities for all of the EPA's environmental-quality-monitoring programs, and management responsibility for demonstration programs. He also integrates EPA-wide efforts for the transfer of technology to private and public groups and evaluates new technologies from the research, development, and demonstration program for their possible carryover to full-scale use by the public after final review by the Science Advisory Board.

The Office of Policy, Planning, and Evaluation is responsible for the overall program-planning activities of the EPA. It develops, initiates, and monitors new and redirected agency programs and goals; prepares reports to the president and the Congress on EPA programs and activities; and develops and monitors interagency agreements.

The Office of Administration and Resource Management is responsible for preparing the agency's budget; financial management and services; fiscal controls; and systems for payroll and disbursement of funds. The assistant administrator in charge of that office also develops and conducts programs for organization and management systems, controls, and services; personnel policies, procedures, and operations; management information systems; data processing management and operations; contracting and obtaining services; grants policies and procedures; and general administrative and support services.

The Office of Enforcement and Compliance Monitoring serves as principal adviser to the administrator in matters pertaining to enforcement of environmental quality standards and regulations, and is responsible for the conduct of enforcement activities on an agency-wide basis. The head of the branch of the OEC known as the Office of Criminal Enforcement and Special Litigation serves as the agency's chief legal prosecutor and works with the Justice Department in legal actions brought against violators of the law.

The Office of the General Counsel serves as the EPA administrator's chief legal adviser and defends the EPA against all lawsuits that are brought before a court.

The Office of the Inspector General (OIG) handles internal investigations and audits. It reviews the EPA's financial transactions, program operations, and administrative activities, and investigates allegations of violations of agency policy or criminal activities by EPA personnel. The inspector general is appointed directly by the president and can be removed only by the president; this allows him to act somewhat independently.

In the Office of External Affairs, the Office of Public Affairs (OPA) serves as principal adviser to the administrator on public affairs aspects of the EPA's activities and programs. The OPA director represents the administrator and the agency in relations with the press, television, radio, and other media and provides public affairs assistance and guidance to all divisions of the EPA. The OPA produces publications, audiovisual materials, and exhibits. It also promotes the development of environmental education programs and prepares and distributes materials on environmental matters to schools, youth groups, and other organizations. The OPA is the agency's principal contact with civic, service, and other groups having an interest in the EPA's mission and activities and responds to general requests for information under the federal Freedom of Information Act.

Also in the Office of External Affairs, the Office of Legislative Analysis (OLA) serves as the adviser to the administrator with respect to legislative and congressional affairs and serves as the major point of congressional contact with the EPA. The director of the OLA advises the administrator and other EPA officials on all legislative proposals originating within or affecting the agency; prepares, reviews, and obtains clearance for proposed legislation and reports on legislation; prepares congressional testimony for EPA officials; and reviews transcripts of congressional hearings. The director cooperates with Congress on EPA activities and, as necessary, maintains liaisons with EPA regional and field officers, other government agencies and departments, and public and private groups having an interest in legislative matters affecting the EPA.

The Office of Federal Activities (OFA) directs the development of national policy for dealing with environmental problems arising from federal facilities and federally authorized or supported activities. The director of the OFA advises the administrator on policy recommendations concerning federal activities to be made to the federal Office of Management and Budget and the Council on Environmental Quality.

EPA Regional Offices

In addition to the agency's national headquarters in Washington, D.C., the EPA has 10 regional offices scattered around the country. The regions and

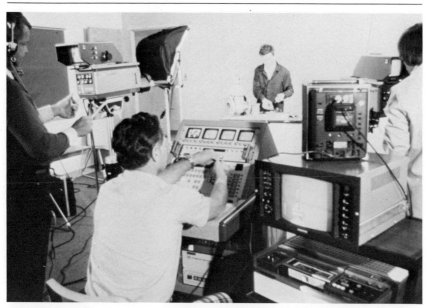

The EPA's Office of Public Affairs produces television programs that provide the public with information about the agency and methods for controlling pollution.

The Offices of Enforcement and General Counsel both serve the EPA as legal advisers. However, their roles are completely separate: Enforcement prosecutes violators of environmental law, and General Counsel defends the agency in lawsuits brought against it.

their offices are located as follows:

- Region 1. New England—Boston
- Region 2. New York-New Jersey—New York City
- Region 3. Middle Atlantic—Philadelphia
- Region 4. Southeast—Atlanta
- Region 5. Great Lakes—Chicago
- Region 6. South Central—Dallas
- Region 7. Central—Kansas City
- Region 8. Mountain—Denver
- Region 9. West—San Francisco
- Region 10. Northwest—Seattle.

The administrators of these regional offices are the EPA's chief representatives in contact with state and local governments and environmental agencies, as well as industry, and other public and private groups. Their main responsibilities involve implementing EPA policies and programs in their regions: To do so, they develop and submit to the EPA Office of Regional Operations local programs for reducing the contamination of the environment.

How the EPA Works

Despite the changes that have occurred in the EPA's organization, funding, and influence since its creation, the agency retains much of its original role. Now, as in the beginning, the EPA's primary functions are to establish and enforce national standards for air and water quality and for individual pollutants; monitor and analyze the environment; conduct environmental research and demonstration projects; and help state and local governments set up and finance pollution control programs. Probably its most important function involves antipollution regulations. How does it fulfill its responsibilities in this area?

The EPA, like any other regulatory agency, operates on the standards-and-enforcement approach to regulation, sometimes called "command and control." Basically, this means that it first sets standards or rules, then checks to make sure people follow these rules and regulations. This method involves four fundamental phases: setting goals, establishing criteria, determining standards (both quality and emissions), and enforcing regulations.

Goal Setting

The first step in setting up any EPA regulatory program is taken when Congress decides to address a specific pollution problem. Being a democratically elected body, Congress typically acts in response to public pressure— when enough Americans express their concern about a problem and their desire to see it fixed. It was such public pressure, as embodied in the politically powerful environmental movement of the late 1960s and early 1970s, that actually spurred the creation of the EPA, along with the important environmental laws—the Clean Air Act, Clean Water Act, and others—passed in the 1970s.

Once enough congressmen become motivated to address a particular pollution issue, they start to think in terms of programs and goals for these programs. Typically, these goals are broad and vaguely worded. For example, the principal stated goal of the Clean Air Act is to protect public health and safety by reducing air pollution; that of the Clean Water Act is to make all the nation's surface waters "fishable and swimmable."

Although such broadly stated goals have little worth in antipollution regulation, they do provide a starting point for investigating such regulation and set the tone for the type and direction of eventual legislation. They also send political messages. The goal of the Clean Water Act, for instance, sent a clear message to the American people and to water polluters that Congress was now serious about securing clean water and would take decisive steps to do so.

Criteria

In order to move from broad goals to specific legislation, Congress needs to understand the exact nature of the particular pollution problem. It needs accurate, reliable scientific data indicating what pollutants are associated with environmental damage and how they cause such damage. From these data, criteria—that is, standards for evaluation and judgment—can be developed to give Congress some idea of what pollutant levels can be allowed while still ensuring good air and water quality. These criteria must be established for

In the wake of an EPA enforcement action, this Indiana steel plant installed equipment to reduce emissions from its smokestacks. Many companies would rather buy expensive antipollution devices than pay costly fines.

each pollutant and for various combinations of pollutants. For example, if Congress intends to protect public health from air pollution, it must know what types and levels of pollutants—such as carbon monoxide and sulfur dioxide—create a public health risk. In the same vein, if Congress wants to restore fish to freshwater lakes, it needs to understand how much pollution the fish can tolerate.

EPA research scientists, working in the field and in laboratories, provide many of these criteria. But this is not an easy task. Data on the environmental effects of many pollutants is sketchy and often totally lacking, and may take years of intense and costly research to determine. Even when criteria have been published, they are often controversial, depending on who is affected by them. For instance, the president of a plastics manufacturing company that discharges wastewater into a river may not feel the same about water quality criteria as a fisherman who sees dead fish in that river, where years before he easily caught the number of fish he needed.

With such limitations on criteria, EPA and Congress often must act on the best information available, even though certain data may be open to scientific criticism.

Quality Standards

Goals and criteria set the stage for the real core of antipollution legislation, and one of the major purposes of the EPA—establishing quality standards, or the maximum allowable levels of pollutants in the environment. This process determines what the EPA, Congress, and the American public consider to be "pollution." For instance, water never has been and never will be totally pure—some levels of contaminants, biological or chemical, will always be present. But the EPA has set quality standards for most individual waste contaminants (and many combinations of contaminants). It has determined, through study and experience, at what levels these contaminants will cause damage to human health and the environment as a whole. Any levels beyond these are considered pollution.

A good set of quality standards specifies the kinds of contaminants to be regulated and the variations of levels and combinations that will be tolerated. In the United States, setting such standards is ultimately a political decision. Congress and the EPA must take many different factors into consideration, both environmental and economic, for every environmental regulation has vast economic implications. A difference of a few parts per million of a pollutant may not have much measurable environmental impact, but it can mean perhaps millions of dollars in pollution control equipment for business and industry.

Emissions Standards

Quality standards are unreachable without limits on the emitters of pollution such as industrial smokestacks, auto exhaust systems, and wastewater discharge pipes. Effective emissions standards clearly indicate the limits on pollution levels needed to meet previously set quality standards.

But setting such standards has become a highly controversial process. For example, once the EPA had set national ambient air quality standards in the Clean Air Act Amendments of 1972, each state was required to calculate the total amount of air pollutants within its various air sheds, and then to assign emission controls to each contributor of pollution in each of these air sheds to ensure that the overall air cleanup goal was met. (An air shed is the total air supply over a specified geographic area.) To do so, the state had to know how much pollution was coming from each source, and how much each source had to reduce its emissions to meet standards. Understandably, this has proven to be an almost impossible task.

Many industrial and business interests, recognizing the relationship between quality standards and emissions standards, fight against both in an attempt to avoid or reduce their legal responsibility. And because it is often difficult to determine exactly who is responsible for what amount of pollution, they often succeed. Regulated industries often base their complaints on the high cost of required pollution-control devices. For example, utility companies and the EPA have been arguing about smokestack scrubbers—devices that remove sulfur dioxide from air emissions—for more than a decade. The EPA imposed the use of these scrubbers after they were developed to meet standards instituted by the Clean Air Act. But, declaring that the scrubbers are inefficient, unreliable, and too costly, the utility companies have resisted installing them until forced to do so.

Enforcement

The EPA enforces environmental regulations through a combination of civil and criminal penalties, including compliance and prohibition orders, fines, and imprisonment. Compliance orders, which require that persons or states follow the requirements of the regulations, and prohibition orders, which require that these persons or states stop any actions that violate the regulations, are the most commonly used enforcement tools. The EPA also can bring suit in federal court to force individual companies to comply with the regulations.

Whatever the method, EPA enforcement must be strong enough to command the respect of those subject to regulation. Effective enforcement involves several characteristics: it requires EPA and state officials to act quickly—immediately in the case of emergencies—to control pollution; it needs to carry sufficiently severe penalties to encourage compliance; and it cannot allow public officials or polluters to evade their responsibilities under the law.

But in the end, an effective pollution control program depends more on voluntary compliance with regulations than on EPA enforcement procedures. The EPA simply does not have enough time, money, or personnel to monitor every potential polluter for noncompliance or to take action against every violation. And because court action is often a slow and inefficient means of enforcement, the EPA usually prefers to negotiate directly with the polluter to address the problem rather than to become involved in lengthy legal disputes. Thus, enforcement often involves "making deals." Armed with a variety of flexible enforcement options, the EPA is in a position to bargain with polluters and to select the enforcement approaches that best fit the individual situation.

This bargaining and negotiating is fundamentally a political process, and as such is subject to political influence. This situation can cause many problems. Conflicts between the EPA and state environmental agencies can cause delay and confusion, as can conflicts between the EPA and other federal agencies that have some environmental responsibilities, such as the Departments of Agriculture and the Interior. Powerful business and industrial influences exert constant pressure on their congressmen for regulatory relief—relaxation of the particular regulations that affect them. And, perhaps most importantly, the EPA is subject to strong influence from the president and his administration. To a great extent, the agency's direction and effectiveness depend on the president and his policies. A president with a strong commitment to environmental protection, such as Richard Nixon in the early 1970s, makes the EPA powerful and effective; but a president, such as Ronald Reagan, for whom environmental regulations seem to represent an economic hindrance, can seriously damage the EPA's ability to do its job.

A polluted beach along Lake Erie. Although the 1972 Clean Water Act Amendments were aimed at eliminating pollution in the nation's waterways, many lakes still cannot be used for recreational activities.

SIX

The Problems Continue

In the years since the EPA came into being in 1970, some progress has been made in controlling pollution, particularly in its most visible and obvious forms. According to the Council on Environmental Quality, total emissions of the 5 major air pollutants decreased by 21 percent during the years 1970 through 1980. This decrease caused air quality to improve in many areas of the country.

However, the EPA has not achieved many of the goals it set in the 1970s. All the nation's waters are not "fishable and swimmable," the stated goal of the Clean Water Act. With some notable exceptions, such as the Great Lakes and the Hudson River, national water quality has not improved greatly over the years. Many U.S. cities still do not have adequate, secondary sewage-treatment plants, and little has been done to address nonpoint sources of water pollution. Despite the Safe Drinking Water Act of 1974 and the Resource Conservation and Recovery Act of 1976, groundwater contamination continues. Smog continues to plague our large cities and industrial centers. And some of the other pollution problems—particularly acid rain and hazardous waste—are becoming more evident, more widespread, and more difficult to control. Although the Superfund program is a needed first step in toxic-waste control and cleanup, it has been badly managed and has accomplished only a small fraction of its original goals.

The lack of progress in many areas of pollution control reflects both the enormous scope of the problem and the complexity of trying to successfully deal with it. The EPA was given a monumental task when it was created in 1970 and has struggled to meet the challenge in the years since.

But this challenge involves many complex factors. We know, at least in a general way, what causes pollution problems. Although some have natural origins, most can be traced directly to human activity. As the population continues to grow, industrial production grows—and so does pollution. Despite the great advances in pollution control technology, new pollution problems continue to plague our industrial society.

But the actual seriousness of the threat posed by pollution is the subject of intense debate. On the one hand, some people see danger in almost every technological development of the modern world, and they predict increasing hazards in the decades to come. On the other hand, there are those who,

An aerial view of Dallas, Texas. Despite the achievements of the EPA, residents in large, densely populated cities continue to cope with problems of smog, litter, and noise pollution.

although admitting that some problems exist, either consider the danger to be much less than is feared, or argue that things that cause pollution (such as nuclear power plants and agricultural pesticides), must be considered in the light of the overall benefits they provide to society.

Various scientific studies provide evidence to support both points of view. And the EPA, a politically influenced body, has to take both sides into account. The agency struggles to find a workable compromise between environmentalists' desires for a pollution-free environment and the political necessity of continued economic growth.

In the 1970s, this compromise was more easily attained. As the decade unfolded, the EPA moved from a single-minded concern with an environmentalist position to a more politically effective approach based on balance and compromise. By working with an environmentally committed Congress, it was able to achieve unprecedented gains in environmental regulation. And by compromising when necessary with powerful business and industrial interests, who complained (often justifiably) about the complexity of the regulations and the high costs of required pollution-control technologies, it was able to implement many of the regulations. Despite many difficulties, more than 90 percent of the nation's industries had some type of antipollution program in place by the decade's end.

But the election of President Ronald Reagan in 1980 brought the dawn of a new era to the EPA and the process of environmental regulation. Under the Reagan administration's "guidance," the agency systematically relaxed certain pollution standards, granted many extensions on compliance deadlines, and generally weakened the strong thrust of environmental regulation that had been built up in the 1970s. Beset by scandal and uncertainty, the EPA lost much of its prestige and effectiveness during the early 1980s.

Today, the EPA stands somewhere between its heyday in the 1970s and the dark days of 1982–83. Its future direction depends mostly on politics. Because the president appoints (and can fire) the EPA director, he has direct control over the agency. President Reagan, responding to the strong desire of the American people for a clean, safe environment, has interfered little with the EPA's programs during his second term in office. As a result, the agency has been able to regain some of its lost momentum.

But what about future presidents? What direction will they give the agency? Of course, it is impossible to predict the future. But with so many serious pollution problems facing us in the decades to come, a strong national program to address these issues—spearheaded by a persistent, effective EPA—is something we cannot afford to be without.

Environmental Protection Agency

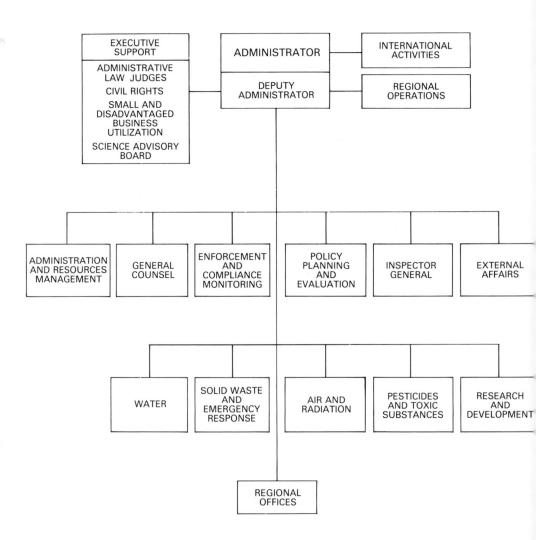

GLOSSARY

acid rain   The combination in the atmosphere of sulfur dioxide, nitrogen dioxide, and water vapor, formed primarily by burning fossil fuels and from automobile exhaust. Acid rain contaminates ponds and lakes, speeds erosion of buildings in cities, and possibly destroys crops and trees.

air shed   The total air supply over a specific geographic area.

aquifer   A large body of groundwater. Aquifers are the main source of drinking water in the United States.

conservation   The preservation of natural resources and the efforts to manage them wisely to prevent the destruction of the environment.

contaminant   Any unhealthy chemical or particle that pollutes the soil, air, or water.

emissions   Substances discharged into the air by sources such as smoke-stacks and automobile exhausts.

fossil fuels   Fuels, such as coal, natural gas, and oil, that are formed in the earth from plant or animal remains and are therefore limited resources.

half-life   The amount of time required for a radioactive substance to lose half of its radioactivity.

hazardous waste   Waste products containing dangerous bacteriological, chemical, or radioactive substances.

nonbiodegradable   Incapable of being decomposed by natural biological processes.

ozone   A form of oxygen that occurs in the upper atmosphere and pro-tects the earth from harmful ultraviolet rays. Ozone also appears as a haz-ardous substance in the lower atmosphere and is a major component of smog.

point pollution   Pollution that comes from a specific, identifiable source, such as a factory. Nonpoint pollution, such as runoff from city streets, comes from an indeterminate source.

pollution   The contamination of the natural environment by human activities that produce wastes and upset the ecological balance.

smog   An unhealthy combination of smoke and fog that occurs in large cities and industrial areas as the result of automobile exhaust and industrial smoke reacting with components of the natural atmosphere.

total suspended particulates (TSP)   Particles of soot and smoke that contribute to air pollution and can cause respiratory problems in animals and humans.

SELECTED REFERENCES

Congressional Quarterly Inc. *Environment and Health.* Washington, D.C.: Congressional Quarterly Service, 1981.

Gilbreath, Kent, ed. *Business and the Environment: Toward Common Ground.* 2nd ed. Washington, D.C.: The Conservation Foundation, 1984.

Kazis, Richard, and Richard L. Grossman *Fear at Work: Job Blackmail, Labor and the Environment.* New York: Pilgrim Press, 1982.

Kerbec, Matthew J., ed. *Your Government and the Environment.* Arlington, Virginia: Output Systems Corp., 1971.

National Commission on Air Quality. *To Breathe Clean Air.* Washington, D.C.: U.S. Government Printing Office, 1981.

Rosenbaum, Walter A. *Environmental Politics and Policy.* Washington, D.C.: CQ Press, 1985.

Sullivan, Julie, ed. *The American Environment.* New York: H. W. Wilson, 1984.

United States Environmental Protection Agency. *Environmental Outlook 1980.* Washington, D.C.: EPA, 1980.

————. *Who's Who in EPA.* Washington, D.C.: EPA, 1985.

United States Environmental Protection Agency, Office of Public Affairs. *EPA Journal.* Published monthly in Washington, D.C.

Vig, Norman J., and Michael E. Kraft, eds. *Environmental Policy in the 1980s: Reagan's New Agenda.* Washington, D.C.: CQ Press, 1984.

INDEX

Acid rain, 21, 25, 27, 71, 85
Agriculture, U.S. Department
 of, 38, 48, 51, 83
Air pollution, 23–26, 37, 41, 43,
 54–57, 62–63, 85
Air Pollution Control Act, 43
Air Quality Act, 43
American Forestry Association,
 38
Aquifers, 30
Arsenic, 29
Asbestos, 25, 56
Atomic Energy Commission, 50
Automobile exhaust, 24, 56

Benzene, 71
Beryllium, 25, 56
Burford, Anne Gorsuch, 68, 69,
 70, 71
Bush, George, 66

Cadmium, 29
Canada, 26, 27
Carbon monoxide, 24, 43, 56,
 57
Carson, Rachel, 39
Carter, Jimmy, 35, 63
CERCLA. *See* Superfund
Chlorofluorocarbons, 26
Chromium, 29
Citizens Advisory Committee
 on Environmental Quality,
 45
Civilian Conservation Corps, 38
Clean Air Act, 17, 43, 44, 62,
 79
Clean Air Act Amendments,
 53, 54, 62
Clean Water Act, 17, 60, 63,
 64, 79, 80, 85
Clean Water Act Amendments,
 59, 63

Commerce, U.S. Department of,
 50, 75
Commoner, Barry, 27
Comprehensive Environmental
 Response, Compensation,
 and Liability Act
 (CERCLA). *See* Superfund
Congress, U.S., 17, 19, 40, 41,
 44, 46, 48, 49, 53, 57, 58, 59,
 60, 62, 63, 65, 79, 80, 81
Conservation, 37, 38, 39
Cooper, James Fenimore, 37
Copper, 29
Costle, Douglas, 63, 68
Council on Environmental
 Quality (CEQ), 47, 48, 51,
 68, 85
Criteria air pollutants, 24–25
Cyanide, 29

Earth Day (1970), 39
Ecological balance, 21
Elizabeth, New Jersey, 33
Emissions control, 57, 63, 67, 82
Environmental laws, 41, 42, 43,
 44, 46, 53, 58, 59, 60, 62, 64,
 66
Environmental movement, 39,
 62, 79
Environmental Protection
 Agency
 achievements of, 19, 85
 administrative history of,
  42–47
 antipollution regulations
  air pollution, 24–25, 55,
   56, 57
  drinking water quality,
   60
  hazardous waste, 15–17,
   60, 61, 64–66

noise pollution, 57, 59
pesticides, 59
solid waste, 57, 58
water pollution, 29, 59
budget cuts to, 17, 68
creation of, 17, 37, 48
decline under Reagan administration, 66–71, 87
emergency action by, 15, 16, 17, 65, 66
Love Canal and, 35
regional offices of, 78
role of, 17, 48, 50, 51, 54, 64, 66, 75, 79, 81, 82, 83, 87
structure of, 73–77
Superfund program, 17, 53, 65
Environmental Quality Council (EQC), 45

Federal Environmental Pesticide Control Act, 59
Federal Insecticide, Fungicide, and Rodenticide Act, 17, 59
Federal Radiation Council, 51
Federal Water Pollution Control Act, 42
Federal Water Pollution Control Act Amendments, 58
Federal Water Pollution Control Administration, 42
Finch, Robert H., 43
Florio, James J., 71
Food and Drug Administration (FDA), 51
Forest Service, U.S., 38
Fossil fuels, 23, 25

Garbage. *See* Solid waste
Gorsuch, Anne. *See* Burford, Anne Gorsuch

Hazardous waste, 15, 16, 19, 31–35, 53, 60, 63–66, 71, 85. *See also* Nuclear waste

Health, Education and Welfare, U.S. Department of (HEW), 42, 43, 44, 50
Hickel, Walter J., 43
Hooker Chemicals and Plastics Corporation, 34
Hydrocarbons, 24, 26, 43, 56, 57

Interior, U.S. Department of the, 41, 43, 44, 48, 50, 51, 83
International Water Supply and Sanitation Decade, 29

Jackson, Henry M., 47
Jefferson, Thomas, 37

Lavelle, Rita, 69
Lead, 25, 29
Love Canal, New York, 33–35, 64

McCloskey, Paul, 39
Mercury, 25, 56

National ambient air quality standards (NAAQS), 56, 63
National Contingency Plan, 65
National emission standards for hazardous air pollutants (NESHAPS), 56
National Environmental Policy Act (NEPA), 46, 47, 48
National Oceanic and Atmospheric Administration (NOAA), 49, 50
National Wildlife Federation, 38
Nelson, Gaylord, 39
Nitrogen dioxide, 24, 26, 27
Nixon, Richard M., 17, 40, 45, 46, 47, 48, 49, 55, 57, 58, 59, 83
Noise Abatement and Control, Office of, 57
Noise Control Act, 17, 59
Noise pollution, 19, 55, 59
Nonpoint pollution, 31, 85

Nuclear waste, 32. *See also* Hazardous waste

Ozone, 24, 25, 26
Ozonosphere, 21, 25, 26

Pesticides, 22, 51, 59, 67
Plutonium, 32
Point pollution, 30
Polychlorinated biphenyls (PCBs), 22, 29, 61
Presidential Task Force on Regulatory Relief, 66, 67
Public Health Service, 42, 43, 48

Radioactive waste. *See* Hazardous waste; Nuclear waste
Reagan, Ronald, 17, 66, 67, 68, 69, 83, 87
Recycling, 57
Resource Conservation and Recovery Act (RCRA), 17, 60, 64, 85
Resource Recovery Act, 53, 57
Rivers and Harbors Act of 1899, 41, 58
Rockefeller, Laurance S., 46
Roosevelt, Theodore, 38
Ruckelshaus, William D., 49, 53, 69, 70, 71

Safe Drinking Water Act, 17, 60, 85
Santa Barbara oil spill, 44, 45

Science Advisory Board, 75
Sierra Club, 38, 48
Silent Spring (Carson), 39
Smog, 21, 24, 25, 85
Soil Conservation Service, 38
Solid waste, 44, 57
Solid Waste Disposal Act, 44
Sulfur dioxide, 24, 27, 43, 71
Superfund, 17, 53, 65, 66, 69, 85
Surface water, 28, 80

Tennessee Valley Authority, 38
Thomas, Lee M., 71
Thoreau, Henry David, 37
Total suspended particulates (TSP), 24, 43
Toxic Substances Control Act (TOSCA), 17, 60, 61
Train, Russell E., 47, 60

United Nations, 29, 74
Uranium, 32
U.S. Agency for International Development (AID), 29

Vinyl chloride, 25, 56

Water pollution, 28–31, 37, 41, 42, 43, 58, 59, 63, 85
Water Pollution Control Act, 41
Water Quality Act, 43
Watt, James, 68

Youngstown, Florida, 33

Kevin J. Law was the publications director for the largest environmental engineering consulting firm in Pennsylvania, where he had contact with the U.S. EPA and with state and local environmental regulatory agencies. Currently he is a free-lance writer and editor specializing in science and health topics and lives in rural Pennsylvania with his wife and two daughters.

Arthur M. Schlesinger, jr., served in the White House as special assistant to Presidents Kennedy and Johnson. He is the author of numerous acclaimed works in American history and has twice been awarded the Pulitzer Prize. He taught history at Harvard College for many years and is currently Albert Schweitzer Professor of the Humanities at the City College of New York.